W9-BCX-748

Parents' Guide to
# Raising
# Responsible
# Kids

Also in the Children's Television Workshop
Family Living Series


*Parents' Guide to Raising Kids Who Love to Learn:*
*Infant to Grade School*


*Parents' Guide to Feeding Your Kids Right:*
*Birth Through Teen Years*


*Parents' Guide to Understanding Discipline:*
*Infancy Through Preteen*


*Parents' Guide to Raising Kids*
*in a Changing World:*
*Preschool Through Teen Years*

## CTW
# FAMILY LIVING SERIES™

Parents' Guide to

# Raising Responsible Kids

## Preschool Through Teen Years

• • • • • • • • • • • • • • • •

**CHILDREN'S TELEVISION WORKSHOP**

Written by Karyn Feiden

Preface by Bill Cosby, Ed.D.

PRENTICE
HALL
PRESS

• • • • • • • • • • • • • • • •

New York • London • Toronto • Sydney
Tokyo • Singapore

CHILDREN'S TELEVISION WORKSHOP
Chairman, Chief Executive Committee: Joan Ganz Cooney
President—Chief Executive Officer: David V. B. Britt
Publisher: Nina Link

Series Editor: Marge Kennedy
Senior Editor: Sima Bernstein
Child Development Consultant: Istar Schwager, Ph.D.
Writer: Karyn Feiden

 PRENTICE HALL PRESS
15 Columbus Circle
New York, NY 10023

Copyright © 1991 by Children's Television Workshop
Line illustrations copyright © 1991 Martha Campbell

PRENTICE HALL PRESS and colophons are registered trademarks of
Simon & Schuster Inc.

Library of Congress Cataloging-in-Publication Data

Feiden, Karyn.
    Parents' guide to raising responsible kids : preschool through teen
years / Children's Television Workshop; written by Karyn
Feiden; preface by Bill Cosby, Ed.D.,—1st ed.
        p.   cm.—(CTW family living series)
    Includes index.
    ISBN 0-13-650813-8
    1. Child rearing—United States. 2. Responsibility.
3. Discipline in children—United States.  I. Children's Television
    Workshop.  II. Title.  III. Title: Raising responsible kids.  IV. Series:
    Children's Television Workshop family living series.
    HQ769.F32  1990
    649".1—dc20                                                      90-47778
                                                                          CIP

Designed by Virginia Pope-Boehling

Manufactured in the United States of America

10  9  8  7  6  5  4  3  2  1

First Edition

# Acknowledgments

• • • • • •

The staff at the Children's Television Workshop wishes to thank Toni Sciarra of Prentice Hall Press for the knowledge and assistance she offered in preparing and editing this series. We also wish to acknowledge the many contributions of Bill Cosby, Ed.D., our preface writer; our advisory panel; the writer of this volume, Karyn Feiden; and researchers, Judith Rovenger and Nancy DeSa.

# Advisory Panel

• • • • • •

ELAINE HEFFNER, Ed.D., is a senior lecturer of education in psychiatry at Cornell University Medical College in New York City, and is program supervisor of the Nursery School Treatment Center at New York Hospital's Payne Whitney Clinic. She is the author of *Mothering: The Emotional Experience of Motherhood after Freud and Feminism* (Doubleday). Dr. Heffner is in private practice in New York City.

ISTAR SCHWAGER, Ph.D., is an educational psychologist, writer, and consultant. She assists in the development of television shows, books, magazines, toys, and other products for parents and children. She is the former director of research of the Children's Television Workshop Magazine Group, and as such helped launch the *Sesame Street Magazine Parents' Guide*. She currently writes a monthly column for that publication on activities for parents and children.

RONALD W. TAFFEL, Ph.D., is the founder and director of the family and couples treatment service at the Institute for Contemporary Psychotherapy in New York City. Formerly the director of treatment of child and adolescent psychiatry at the Downstate Medical Center, he has been a child and family therapist for 20 years. Dr. Taffel has taught and written extensively about family therapy. He has been one of the most popular speakers on parenting matters in the New York City area, giving hundreds of talks to parent groups. He lives in New York City with his wife and daughter.

# About the Preface Writer

· · · · · ·

BILL COSBY, Ed.D., is the creator and star of "The Cosby Show," one of the most popular and influential series on television. His television career began with the 1960s series *I Spy*, for which he received three Emmy Awards. He has since starred in additional series and television specials, including "Children's Theater" and Children's Television Workshop's "The Electric Company." He has authored three bestselling books: *Fatherhood*, *Time Flies*, and *Love and Marriage*. With more than 25 years in comedy, Dr. Cosby has also produced several albums, five of which have won Grammy Awards for Best Comedy Album. He is presently producing and co-writing a series of jazz albums. The father of five children, Dr. Cosby and his wife, Camille, are involved in several charity and philanthropic organizations and have made generous contributions to several predominantly black colleges to promote education. Dr. Cosby is also an active trustee of his alma mater, Temple University in Philadelphia.

# About the Author

• • • • • •

KARYN FEIDEN is a New York City–based freelance writer and editor with extensive credits in the fields of health and education. She is the author of *Hope and Help for the Chronic Fatigue Syndrome* (Prentice Hall Press) and *Indoor Pollution* (Ballantine) and is a contributor to The Children's Television Workshop Family Living Series book *Parents' Guide to Raising Kids Who Love to Learn* (Prentice Hall Press).

# Series Introduction

• • • • • •

**W**hat do children need to learn about themselves and the world around them if they are to realize their potential? What can parents do to facilitate their children's emotional, physical, and intellectual growth?

For more than a generation, the Children's Television Workshop (CTW), creator of *Sesame Street*, has asked these questions and has conducted extensive research to uncover the answers. We have gathered together some of the best minds in child development, health, and communication. We have studied what experts around the world are doing to nurture this generation. And, most important, we have worked with children and parents to get direct feedback on what it means to be a productive and fulfilled family member in our rapidly changing world. We recognize that there are no simple solutions to the inherent complexities of child rearing and that in most situations there are no single answers that apply to all families. Thus we do not offer a "how-to" approach to being a parent. Rather, we present facts where information will help each of you make appropriate decisions, and we offer strategies for finding solutions to the various concerns of individual families.

The development of the CTW Family Living Series is a natural outgrowth of our commitment to share what we have learned with parents and others who care for today's children. It is hoped that the information presented here will make the job of parenting a little easier—and more fun.

# Contents

• • • • • •

# CONTENTS

## PART III • What's Next?

# Preface

If you're a parent like me, you must have wished there had been a book like this one available a long time ago. Raising a responsible child is not easy. In fact, it is often maddening. As a father of five, I know whereof I speak. I make no claim to having been the so-called primary caretaker. Camille, my wife, was the one who was there for the children while I was away from home a lot functioning as the breadwinner. However, I was an involved father who participated in the care of the kids as often as my schedule would allow because I like kids. It is as a parent, not as a self-appointed sociologist or psychologist, that I write this preface. Whatever wisdom I may—or may not—possess on the subject of children is mostly derived from common sense and experience. So hear me out, even if my tongue sometimes seems to be tucked solidly in the side of my cheek.

No matter how much love you give your kids, you still have the endlessly difficult job of trying to get them to do the right thing: to be responsible in and out of school, and at work and at play.

For example, no moment in parenting is more distressing than when your child, who has gone to stay at someone else's home, forgets to call you. It's not easy to forget to make such a call, because you have reminded him nine times that he should do it, but he manages to forget nonetheless.

One weekend my oldest daughter left home to visit a friend who lived about 30 miles away. I missed her terribly, of course, and I also wondered if she had arrived safely, so I called her.

"Hey, Dad," she said, warming my heart by remembering who I was.

"Honey, I just wanted to make sure you were safe," I said.

"Of *course*."

"But I didn't *know*."

"Oh, yeah. I forgot."

"Well, the next time I'll just leave it up to the state police, okay? I'll just have them call me and let me know that you arrived. I'm sure they have a service like that for frantic fathers."

"Oh, Dad, that's not fair."

"True. I told you fewer than 10 times to call me, so you may have missed the message. You see, all I want to know is that you got someplace safely—someplace far away, that is. It doesn't count for local trips. I mean, you don't have to call and say, 'Dad, I made it to the bank.' Wait a minute—I see what happened: You forgot our number."

But then I realized that she couldn't have forgotten our number because it was the one she called for money. Her trips to the bank are just walks to my den.

What is equally maddening about your child's visit to a distant friend is the call you get from the friend's mother or father telling you how lovely and helpful your child has been.

"I just can't tell you what a polite young gentleman he is," the mother says. "He straightened his room and made his bed and even offered to do the dishes."

At moments like these, you truly feel that you have fallen down the rabbit hole. You wonder if all your teaching has borne some fruit after all, or whether your child is purposely trying to drive you insane. Maybe at times like these I needed to consult a manual—like this book. Or perhaps I should have resorted to good old-fashioned discipline, except that I don't know exactly what that is, or even if it would work in trying to get little ones (and big ones) to do the right thing.

You see, raising a responsible child is not just about discipline. It is about much, much more and has a lot to do with values—good values—that instill in children a sense of caring about others, taking on their share of chores, and knowing how to cooperate with others (particularly their parents, I must add). This means turning your child, who comes into this world rather uncivilized, into a respectable (or is that respected) citizen.

Indeed, how responsible a child becomes is, at least in part, a function of the parents' own values and expectations. Sometimes the hardships of life and a tough environment make it doubly hard for mothers and fathers to foster their hopes for their children. I grew up in a neighborhood in Philadelphia where things were so tough that many parents felt thankful if their children simply stayed out of trouble with the law and didn't go to jail. Yet parents must continue to do the best they can, even when outside circumstances seem bleak.

Children from all walks of life watch and imitate their parents. Youngsters are wise; they pick up the real messages and values and are much more concerned with what you do than with what you say.

So the first and most important task in raising a responsible child is for parents to teach reasonable social values by word and demonstrate a sense of responsibility by deed in the way they conduct their own lives. Children will not respect parents who say one thing and do another. This has always been true but may even be more relevant today, when citizens are demanding better and higher standards of ethical behavior from private and public officials, from leaders and mentors.

For example, it is hard for you to convince your child that it is important to be punctual if you are always late or your bill payments are always past due. And an inherent question of children whose parents violate the law is "Why should I be law-abiding?" Similarly, a parent who abuses drugs, alcohol, and cigarettes is not a good model for responsible conduct. It should not surprise anyone that such parents face great obstacles in raising a responsible child.

Yet many parents commit even bigger mistakes by resorting to the excessive use of physical violence in trying to discipline—reasoning, from their vantage point, that they have a better chance at raising a mature person. Their approach backfires more often than not because most children who are so abused become angry, bitter, and rebellious. Worse still, many maltreated kids themselves become violent toward parents, neighbors, and their community, a state of affairs that no one welcomes. I regret the time I struck my own son in anger.

There are good reasons to avoid the use of physical force, foremost among them being that such a method is detrimental to raising a healthy citizen. Your child may initially appear to accept the discipline, but it may only be on the surface. Children sometimes behave or submit to authority when assaulted but may not *internalize the values* that help them to become disciplined and responsible on their own. To raise responsible children, it is critical, in my opinion, that their behavior truly emanate from inside them because they, with their parents' guidance, have to make up their own minds to embrace decent values and self-discipline. If their apparent responsible behavior comes entirely from the terror of possible physical abuse, the change may be temporary and other problems can result.

I urge parents to rethink their values about spanking and

to practice new ways of discipline that respect the ability of children to learn and grow. This volume, even though it does not include *discipline* in its title, can open doors for parents who want their children to emerge in this world as good citizens standing on their own two feet. When they become adults and establish their own families, they will be in a fine position to raise the next generation of responsible citizens who, in their turn, will help to make this world a better place.

*Parents' Guide to Raising Responsible Kids* is an excellent book, one from which all parents can learn and all children can thereby benefit.

BILL COSBY, ED.D.

# A Few Words About Pronouns

• • • • • •

The child fell off *his* bike." Or how about "The child fell off *her* bike"? Then again we could say, "The child fell off *his or her* bike." How to deal with pronouns?

If you are a regular reader of *Sesame Street Magazine Parents' Guide,* you know that our policy is to alternate the use of gender-related pronouns. In one paragraph we say *his:* in the following one we use *her.* In a book, that specific policy is not quite as practical—there are just too many paragraphs—but it works in a general way by alternating chapters.

# PART I
......
# Raising a Responsible Child

"I DON'T KNOW WHY I HAVE TO PICK IT UP. I'M NOT RESPONSIBLE FOR THE LAW OF GRAVITY."

# CHAPTER ONE

• • • • • •

# What Is a Responsible Child?

In the popular fairy tale *Pinocchio*, the wooden puppet's nose grew whenever he told a lie. Many parents wish they could depend on such an obvious gauge to determine just how upright their children are. But in today's complex and troubled society—with its rapidly shifting social mores, its splintered families, and a diversity that defies any attempt to impose uniform values—it's sometimes hard even to define for children what moral and responsible behavior is and what the consequences are for behaving irresponsibly. While storybook heroines and heroes are rewarded for kindness, courage, wisdom, hard work, and self-sacrifice, the modern world seems to condone greed, selfishness, cruelty, and a host of other dishonorable traits.

However, the old stories still reflect the kind of responsible behavior most parents want to teach their children. The central themes of responsible behavior *can* be found in contemporary models. A great number of television sitcom families, such as the one depicted in "The Cosby Show," struggle weekly to teach their children to do the right thing. Nonetheless, raising a responsible child today is a more profound and challenging task than any television show can resolve. Almost daily, newspaper headlines shout out stories about teenage drug abuse, unplanned pregnancies, and high dropout rates—tragic testimony to the fact that many young adults have not learned adequate respect for their own minds and bodies, nor have they learned even the basics of good citizenship. Frightening stories about violence in the schools and crime on the street are all sad reminders that alienating and self-destructive behavior and a lack of respect for others are far too common.

Parents, teachers, and anyone else with influence over a child's behavior are inevitably challenged by life's complexities: How do we keep young people safe while providing them room to experiment and grow? What responsibilities are appropriate to assign a child, and what should be done if those responsibilities are not met? What is a proper allowance, and how should its use be monitored? How can we instill a child with our values when so many of his peers come from families with very different values? How should we handle a situation in which we do not trust our child's friends? How can a child best be motivated without being placed under unreasonable pressure? What can be done to encourage a child's cooperation at school? How can a sense of belonging be fostered so that he is able to fulfill his obligations in a democratic society?

There are, of course, no easy answers to any of these questions. Teaching a child to be responsible and to care about himself and others is not like teaching him arithmetic; there is no lesson plan that systematically covers the necessary skills. Nor can responsibility be imposed; punishments and rewards do not force a child to behave appropriately in all situations. And it is clearly impossible to prepare a child for everything he will encounter along life's journey or to monitor his behavior at every moment, especially as he grows older.

A more practical goal and the central theme of this book is to help parents instill in their child *a set of values that will endure beyond parental influence*. These values are conveyed in lessons taught in the home, at school, and in the community, which help a child develop the critical components of responsibility that last a lifetime: good judgment, sound character, and a strong conscience.

As a child takes increasing part in the decisions that shape his life, he gradually gains a sense of control and recognizes that he is the director of what he does and that it is he who will determine how the story of his life unfolds. He learns that the true measure of a human being is not based on winning or losing. Instead, it is in the wisdom gained from experience and in the ability to contribute to others as well as to himself. With this knowledge, a young person can face disappointment and the unpredictable twists of life with courage and a secure sense of his own worth.

## View of Childhood

Many of our notions about child rearing and responsibility are bound by culture, history, and class status. For example, the American passion for individualism contrasts sharply with the Japanese emphasis on group loyalty. Thus in the United States, visible displays of personal ambition are considered appropriate, while in Japan, where "fitting in" is generally the objective, such a drive is thought unseemly. In our country's past, society valued self-denial in the interests of the family and the community, whereas modern society, in general, values loyalty to the self and the ability to improve one's own life. In addition, society once placed the blame for irresponsible and immoral behavior exclusively on the individual, whereas today, the blame is likely to be extended to include the whole of society; the failure of schools, the effects of poverty, and lack of social support systems, more than the individual, are blamed.

In a similar contrast, parental attitudes toward discipline

and what is considered proper behavior have historically swung between strictness and permissiveness. Years ago, British parents were encouraged to lock their children in the closet to stop their impulsive behavior. In the latter part of the nineteenth century, however, a new generation of experts interpreted a child's rebelliousness as a celebration of his liberty. By the late 1960s, on both sides of the Atlantic, permissiveness became even more pronounced as parents were urged to allow children to develop according to their own rules and temperaments. The common belief during this time was that no one should be allowed to restrict an individual's freedom by imposing his own beliefs. For the first time in modern history, parents by and large relinquished their authority. Recently the pendulum appears to be swinging back as more people are urging that restrictions once again be placed on young people, although few recommend that traditional methods of authoritarian discipline be reestablished.

Clearly the definition of responsible behavior is closely tied to the perspective of a particular time and place. Within the past century, people's views of family and children and notions of responsibility have changed more than once. Even in the last 10 years the traditional idea of what constitutes a family has been greatly challenged by the different forms families have taken. The model of an intact family now fits only about a third of families with children. Such changes can leave parents confused about what approach to follow in establishing a sense of family and in conveying values to children.

## Looking Back

The American family as a social and economic unit has changed dramatically in the years since our nation was first settled. Well into the nineteenth century, the United States

was largely an agrarian society, and most communities adhered to fairly similar standards and mores. Families were
largely self-sufficient, producing most of their own food and
clothing and building their own shelters. Relatively few
people sought outside employment, although young boys
might be sent away from home for a few years to learn a
skill as unpaid apprentices. The few items that could not be
produced in the home were generally obtained through
trade.

In those days larger families were preferred. After all, big
families meant more workers to tend the animals, cultivate
the land, and lighten the load of labor-intensive household
responsibilities. The family often extended also to boarders,
unrelated dependents, or young apprentices living in the
home, as well as to relatives who lived nearby.

Everyone in the family had clearly defined and seldom-
challenged roles, with labor usually divided along sex-
segregated lines. Mother was responsible for domestic
duties, including caring for children's needs, making clothes,
preparing food, and tending orchards and gardens. However, she and the children would help with the heavier
work during certain "crisis" times, such as the harvest. Father was head of the household, charged with doing the
heavy farm work and other outdoor tasks. His word was
law in the home. Until the mid-nineteenth century he also
filled the role of moral and educational teacher (using the
Bible as the principal textbook) to the children, who were
seen as inherently bad and in need of discipline, or without
moral tendencies of any kind. At that time women were
considered irrational and unstable. By the 1850s women began to take on a greater degree of moral authority, and the
responsibility for providing guidance to children began its
steady move from being a male duty to a female one.

Because the family working together was essential to economic survival, children from an early age took on signifi-

cant responsibilities. They knew the value of their contribution to the family and the hardship caused if they did not do their assigned duties. Parents taught their children how to run a household and work the land, knowing that such training would later have tangible payoffs in the help children gave. In general, young people of the time had the security of knowing what was expected of them and of understanding the role they played at home and would play as adults in the community.

The nineteenth century brought the Industrial Revolution, which had enormous implications for the family and for society. As the workplace shifted from home to factory, large families became more of an economic liability than an asset. The model of agrarian, self-sufficient families was gradually replaced by urban-based, more isolated nuclear families.

In this new society the role of the father changed to that of a wage earner who went out into the world to make his living. The mother, who assumed sole responsibility for running the household, became increasingly responsible for the moral education of the children. The father no longer had the time to devote to instructing his children; the mother, because she was "uncorrupted" by exposure to the outside world, became society's model of virtue for children, who were now viewed as being born in a state of innocence. The mother consequently was blamed if her children did not live up to accepted standards of morality.

Eventually, it became impractical for children to receive most of their education or religious training at home, and a public school system emerged. With exposure to outside influences, the homogeneous community, comprised of neighbors from similar backgrounds and with shared values, began to disintegrate. At the same time, children's contributions became less crucial to daily survival and their clearly defined role within the family was slowly lost.

## Contemporary Attitudes Toward Childhood

The economic and social changes launched by the Industrial Revolution have continued at a dizzying pace through the twentieth century. Along with redefining how adults live and work, the changes people experienced have caused a radical alteration in their ideas about children.

Children have continued to be viewed with the sentimentality that emerged in the Romantic era of the 1800s. In a pronounced shift from nineteenth-century attitudes, however, many parents have become more permissive in raising their children, requiring few household responsibilities and imposing even fewer limits. This attitude has extended the middle-class American childhood well into a person's 20s, an age that had once been seen as thoroughly adult.

In the absence of a family's economic dependence on young people, children today are often protected and nurtured into their teenage years and beyond. In some families there is the belief that "children should be children as long as they can" or that "completing his homework is the only thing I ask from my child." These are uniquely American attitudes, says psychologist Jerome Kagan in *The Nature of the Child*. "The special ingredient in the American form of child-centeredness," he writes, "is its one-sidedness. Parents are supposed to sacrifice for their children while the children are expected to grow increasingly independent of their parents. For many middle-class families, the child is a beautiful young bird to be cared for until it is ready to fly free in the forest." Children in these families may have trouble coping with adult responsibilities when the carefree days of childhood end.

In other families, however, the beautiful young bird is

caged. These kids are overburdened with enormous and time-consuming responsibilities, including housework and child care. Sometimes this is the sad result of neglect, as busy and self-involved parents cut short the childhood years by asking too much and giving too little. More often it is a reflection of new realities and economic pressures. In many single-parent families, a child's contribution to the running of the household has once again become vital. A child may be expected to care for himself and siblings and to take on household duties that are far beyond his capacity. Many school officials have observed children too tired to participate in class or too busy attending to their basic needs to have time for schoolwork, much less for social activities.

Giving a child too much responsibility obviously can be as damaging as giving him too little. The ideal approach, and one that is encouraged throughout this book, is for parents to be aware of their child's developmental stages and to recognize his ability to put feelings, values, and beliefs into action. By "living" responsibility as well as by teaching it, adults assign *age-appropriate* tasks to their child and encourage him to do his part.

## The Building Blocks of Responsibility

By paying attention and responding to children's growing ability to understand responsibility, adults can help them to assemble the many building blocks of responsibility. In broad terms we can say that a responsible child is one who has a strong sense of self-esteem, empathizes with other human beings, internalizes notions of right and wrong, develops good judgment, understands the consequences of his behavior, and contributes his fair share. In other words, a responsible child respects and values himself, other people, and the environment; helps his neighbors; contributes something in return to the people who give to him; and grows into an adult who confidently and consciously works to help make this a better world. By teaching these values a day at a time, as much by example as by words, most parents are in a good position to raise such a person.

## A Strong Sense of Self-Esteem

Perhaps the most important building block of responsibility is high self-esteem: a deeply felt, positive belief in oneself. As one mother said when asked what she would wish for her children when they grow up, "I want my children to learn that they can stick to their own values. Then they will not be afraid to do things they feel are right. The ability to be independent comes from strong self-esteem."

Psychologist Dorothy Corkille Briggs, author of *Your Child's Self-Esteem*, describes the importance of self-esteem this way: "Your child's judgment of himself influences the kinds of friends he chooses, how he gets along with others, the kind of person he marries, and how productive he will be. It affects his creativity, integrity, stability and even whether he will be a leader or a follower. His feelings of self-worth form the core of his personality and determine the use he makes of his aptitudes and abilities. His attitude toward himself has a direct bearing on how he lives all parts of his life."

A child who has developed a sense of self-esteem has an invaluable foundation to sustain him through life. Confident enough to take chances without being reckless, secure but not arrogant, and unafraid to act differently from the crowd, he is well positioned to define ambitious goals for himself. A child who cares about himself will also care for his body, acknowledge and cope with his emotions, tend to his possessions, and respect others without judging them.

Above all, high self-esteem equips a child to handle the setbacks and disappointments that are an inevitable part of life. Rather than saying, "I guess I'm just no good at basketball," a child who misses a winning point will tell himself, "Boy, I sure blew that game. I'm going to have to practice some more, and next time I'm sure I'll do better." He does not berate himself or view failure as a negative statement on his value as a human being. Nor does he abandon the pursuit of a goal simply because he failed to reach it on the first attempt.

## The Capacity for Empathy

To empathize with another human being is to put oneself in another person's place in order to understand how he feels about something from his point of view. A sense of empathy is crucial to developing a sense of right and wrong, an understanding of how one person's actions affect others, and an awareness of consequences of behavior. The need for empathy has become even greater in today's society, in which self-gratification and material rewards have received such emphasis.

Many child psychologists believe that the capacity for empathy is present at birth, citing the "empathetic distress cry" that is often emitted when one baby hears another crying. Certainly there are many clear-cut examples of an empathetic response in children under the age of two, such as the toddler who offers his security blanket or a favorite toy to soothe his howling baby sister. In later years, children step into the shoes of others by playacting, which allows them to feel someone else's joy, sadness, anger, and pride, and to see situations through the eyes of others.

By the time they become preteens and teenagers, children are able to see situations from others' point of view and understand other people's feelings. They become aware that groups are made up of individuals and that each individual has dreams and problems just as they do.

Parents can be a great influence in guiding their children toward developing empathy. For example, school-age children who make fun of a disabled child can be asked how they would feel if they were called hurtful names. Once they identify with another child's emotional realities, children can learn to respect another's feelings because doing so makes them feel better. They will begin to see a worthwhile person who just happens to have a disability.

## Knowing Right from Wrong

Young children who are just beginning to learn to control their impulses often do what is right to please their parents, to avoid disapproval, or to escape punishment. As children learn more about what is good and bad behavior, they will develop their own standards and begin to act on the basis of inner conviction or conscience. They will behave appropriately whether or not anyone is watching or there is any danger of being caught.

The child who says to himself, "I had better not take a candy bar from the shelf because the store owner may see me and my parents will be angry," operates from a very different perspective than the child who says, "I won't take a candy bar because it's not right to take something that belongs to someone else, and it would be unfair to the store owner." Sooner or later, the first child will stumble across the opportunity to steal without the fear of getting caught, and most likely will succumb to temptation. By contrast, the second child's internal messages and sense of empathy will control his behavior in all situations, whether or not he'd be able to get away with something.

To behave responsibly, a child (or adult) must develop a social awareness that includes recognizing the rights of potential victims of his actions. Taking a candy bar injures the store owner in more ways than an economic one. Trust is broken, preventive security measures add cost to the product, and thus the problem eventually is shared by all the customers. Therefore, the first steps in learning to care for the common good are *to see the consequences of all actions in terms of specific people* and *to care about their viewpoint.* The complexities of the economic system may require a more abstract understanding, but children are capable of learning that the world is made up of individuals.

## Developing Good Judgment

Traditional institutions, such as local community governments, churches, and schools, were once powerful forces for social stability. While still influential, no single institution today is strong enough to define and enforce uniform rules of behavior for all people. Instead, our society depends heavily on the ability of people to exercise good judgment and to make wise decisions for themselves.

Ultimately the ability to make thoughtful decisions is closely tied to integrity and strong personal values. A child who trusts his instincts and has been reassured that his sense of judgment is good is not easily manipulated by others and is not afraid to take a stand. He respects authority figures but does not hesitate to question an order if it conflicts with his own sense of judgment.

In our consumer-oriented society, where what you own is sometimes confused with who you are, exercising good judgment also means buying what you need and personally like, not what the neighbors have or what is in fashion this year. It also means learning street smarts. With children being exposed to a host of dangers at ever-earlier ages, knowing how to respond to a stranger, when to report a relative's too-friendly advances, and how to say no to drugs are all aspects of having good judgment.

Parental respect for children's wise decisions, whether they are made first through imitation or even by coincidence, can help children develop confidence, self-respect, and reason. They will be more willing to try to think things through if their early attempts are encouraged.

## Understanding the Consequences of Behavior

From infancy on, a child discovers how his behavior affects himself and other people. A toddler throws a toy in anger and sees it break. Seven-year-old Sara doesn't meet Kelly at the neighborhood softball game as promised and is bewildered when Kelly won't agree to meet her the following week. Jim, 10, hands in a messy homework assignment and is told he must do it again.

When no one steps in to remedy the situation—by immediately buying a new toy, making excuses for inconsiderate behavior, or accepting sloppy work, for example—a child learns one of the essential pieces of the responsibility puzzle: "I must live with the consequences of my actions and my decisions." By the age of two, and possibly even before, children are able to understand that their behavior can help or hurt themselves and others.

Overprotected children usually fail to learn from their mistakes because they are never forced to face consequences. Only later in life, when parents are no longer available to wave away errors with a magic wand, do they discover the boomerang effect of inconsiderate, unfair, or careless behavior. By then the consequences are likely to be harsher than in childhood. Children who receive meager supervision from parents and other adults also grow up confused about the relationship between behavior and its consequences, which underscores the value of good role models.

Important as it is for children to connect an action with its result, they also must realize that they cannot control everything in life. It is typical, for example, for young children to feel responsible for the breakup of their parents' marriage. "If only I hadn't fought with my brother so much, maybe Daddy wouldn't have left" or "I promise to make my bed every morning if Mommy and Daddy will stop fighting" are often a child's responses to family trauma. As adults, we know that a world of events operates independently of a child, and it is important that we help children recognize the limits of their influence while we help them to take responsibility for situations they *can* control.

## Contributing a Fair Share

Some people are always the first to volunteer when there is work to be done, a neighbor needs help moving, efforts are being organized to clean up a community park, or an elderly person needs help with grocery shopping. Invariably, these people also are reliable and cooperative on the job and are widely respected by their colleagues. They take pride in "doing a fair share" and contributing to their community, and they make this an integral part of their value system.

However, in any group there are usually those who try to avoid work as well. These are people who look for any chance to slip away when the load is heaviest. They are the ones who typically respond to requests for help with: "It's not my job," "I don't have time," and "I did it last month; ask someone else."

Both patterns of behavior are rooted in childhood lessons

about responsibility. Good work habits, which begin as good study habits and a willingness to complete assigned chores, are established early and last a lifetime. The hard-working adult most likely learned as a child that privileges are earned, that delaying gratification is a satisfying way to attain desired goals, and that generosity is rewarding and is generally returned. By contrast, those who avoid contributing often grow up with a sense of entitlement and a lack of concern for others. They fail to realize the satisfying payoffs of commitment and hard work.

When trying to stress the importance of good work habits, however, many parents today may feel they are swimming against the trend toward instant gratification and entitlement. In the face of these difficulties, sometimes the only thing parents can do is to try to convey the idea that a job well done is personally satisfying. They also can point out any incidents reported by the media or occurring in their own community in which hard-working, caring people are rewarded.

## The Stages of a Child's Development

Assembling the building blocks of responsible behavior cannot happen at once but instead occurs gradually in a child's development. The social skills a child is ready to master and the responsibilities he is ready to take on depend greatly on his level of understanding and ability. For example, take the art of getting dressed. A toddler cannot be expected to dress himself, but a healthy six-year-old is fully capable of doing so. By the teenage years, a young person may be selecting his own clothes in a store and perhaps buying them with money he has earned himself. Similarly, a three-year-old cannot be expected to prepare his own breakfast, but it is reasonable to ask a 10-year-old to do so. And while we cannot expect a three-year-old to understand the reasons for rules in a game, most seven-year-olds insist that game rules be followed exactly.

Within a few short years, then, a child moves from complete dependence to having both the sense of responsibility necessary to take care of himself in limited ways and the ability to empathize with the needs of others. How does this process take place? What follows is a general description of a child's social development stages.

## The First Years
## (Birth to Age Five)

In these first years of life, extraordinary growth takes place: A totally dependent infant develops into a child with many social skills, the ability to use language, and a growing sense of autonomy. Although everyone agrees that children develop at different rates, recent studies have shown that children are able at a much earlier age than previously believed to understand and care about other people's feelings and to respond by regulating their own behavior.

In general, infants become attached to their primary care-givers in the first few months through consistent, loving care that is responsive to their needs. Through loving touch, play, and parental talk, infants learn that their existence is pleasurable to others. Before they are a year old, infants are capable of wanting to follow their parents' instructions, such as learning to pet the family dog gently rather than pulling its tail.

When babies become toddlers, they are mobile and excited about exploring and learning. In a world where almost everything and everyone is much larger than they are, toddlers take enormous satisfaction in small accomplishments and can show great frustration in being unable to do things they see older children or adults do. They also are ready to learn about their effect on their world, such as that a ball bounces when they throw it and their knee hurts when they bump it. Toddlers also know that their behavior can have an impact on their parents, and most of them don't want to make their parents unhappy. Thus they are capable of learning limits, such as staying away from a potted plant, even though they may need to be reminded of that limitation many times.

Between the ages of two and three, children become much more independent and may appear to be stuck permanently in the "no" stage. While respecting this need for independence, parents can effectively foster cooperation if they allow their children to practice making appropriate choices. For example, children may be given a choice between two outfits to wear or two foods to eat. Two- and three-year-olds are also capable of understanding that they can hurt other people's feelings, even though they still may not always be willing to share or to treat others nicely.

Three-year-olds are generally more cooperative than two-year-olds. They want to be a part of things and to help around the house. They are also old enough to start learning basic manners, such as saying "please" and "thank-you" and to understand that good manners make others feel good. Playing with other children is very important, and their increased willingness to share helps them make friends. They also are able to understand that refusing to share or treating others badly means that they could be treated the same way in return, although they still have trouble seeing a situation from someone else's point of view.

Four- and five-year-olds often exhibit great identification with their parents and look to them as role models. Children at these ages readily accept parental authority. They try to do what's right to please their parents and to avoid punishment. They also have a need to believe they are valued by their families. Including them in daily chores by having them clean up after themselves and having them help with small jobs such as setting the table encourages a growing personal sense of responsibility, especially if children are praised and reassured that their contributions are helpful.

Four- and five-year-olds also actively test their limits. At this point, consistently enforcing old and new rules and patiently explaining why those rules are important can help young children learn the difference between proper and improper behavior.

One of the most characteristic dimensions of the three-, four- and five-year-olds is a passion for make-believe. During this period, the imagination has free rein. Children are inventive, establishing their own rules for games; impersonating fire fighters, witches, pirates, kings, and queens; talking on magic telephones; enjoying the company of invisible companions; and describing implausible scenarios in vivid detail. To some parents, these exaggerations constitute lying. However, tall tales are most often simply expressions of what young children *wish* were true. Children at these ages are capable of telling and knowing what a lie is. However, they probably will not see anything wrong in telling a lie if it gets them what they want.

## A Greatly Expanding World
### (Ages Six to Nine)

The middle years of childhood are a time of striving for competence and mastery. Adjusting to the demands of school becomes one of the greatest challenges to children at these ages. They also are confronting a wider variety of new children, discovering new ideas about how other families live, learning how to negotiate a wider geographic area, and just beginning to understand large concepts, such as life, love, and death.

Children of these ages have a great sense of independence, which sometimes may take the form of defiance of parents' wishes and a seemingly uncaring attitude toward other people's feelings and other people's property. They are working hard to find their place in the world and to develop a sense of who they are. As a result, they see the world mainly from their own point of view. However, their widening horizons may also result in frequent feelings of insecurity and the need to receive their family's reassurance of their worth. They may also seek approval from other adults, such as teachers and coaches, and from friends their own age.

Because friends are becoming increasingly important, parents of grade-schoolers have a good opportunity to help their children learn what it means to be a friend. They also can teach that friendship has to be earned through trust, fair play, and respect for others' feelings. Children's strong sense of fairness at this age can also be used by parents to teach cooperation and compromise by showing children that other people want fair treatment as much as they do.

Conscience begins to play a larger part in the thinking of school-age children, although fear of being caught rather than an internalized sense of right and wrong still may be the greater deterrent to misbehavior. Children at this age know what's right and wrong—especially when it comes to how fairly *they* are treated—but they may see their own behavior as right no matter what they do if it gets them what they want and they can get away with it. This may lead to lying, cheating, and stealing of household change or small items. To counteract this behavior, parents can work to point out the harmful effects of such behavior on others, such as parental distrust, which children may not have realized. Parents also can reduce their own upset by remembering that such behavior is not uncommon and can be corrected.

## The Preteen Years
## (Ages 10 to 12)

Sometimes viewed as the calm before the storm of adolescence, these years may be marked for parents by increased cooperation and loving companionship from their children. Preteens regulate their own behavior based on *internal* standards of right and wrong rather than from a fear of punishment. They are able to identify with viewpoints other than their own.

Life is far from perfect, however. At this stage cliques begin to form at school and a child's place in the social order is of great concern. Bullies emerge and some youngsters are excluded from the "in crowd." At home children may demonstrate startling viciousness toward their siblings. Just as the stirrings of puberty are first felt, preteens are gaining a measure of real independence, spending long periods of time without parental supervision and doing more solo traveling.

By this stage a child generally makes most of his own decisions about what to wear to school. In fact, some kids are fanatical about their wardrobe. Nonetheless, clothes are often tossed about the room—a pattern consistent with other sloppy habits. Beds go unmade, rooms are messy, and habits of personal cleanliness are often poor, especially for boys. This is also a period when agreed-upon chores don't get completed. A child who is highly responsible about baby-sitting for a neighbor or mowing a neighbor's lawn will likely neglect these same tasks at home.

Best friends, usually of the same sex, become intensely important, along with preteens' own strict rules governing loyalty and fairness. Jealousy and rivalry between friends becomes common. Preteens care more about what other people think of them, often because they are insecure about how they view themselves. They can be especially influenced by what other children say and are allowed to do. At this point, parents are called upon to begin letting go while imposing certain limits, which children still greatly need. This is a time when parents compete with peer groups for influence over their child.

## Early to Midadolescence
## (Ages 13 to 16)

Enormous physical and emotional changes are taking place at this stage, including increased interest in and confusion about sex. Teenagers may be highly critical of themselves and suffer extreme self-consciousness in trying to deal with the body changes that have overtaken them.

In general, teenagers are relatively independent and able to schedule their own time responsibly. By age 16 more than likely they will get their first chance to perform paid work outside the home—a responsibility that is central to adult life. Chores will be expanded at home, but many teens also baby-sit, mow lawns, have newspaper routes, or work part-time in stores to earn their own money. Access to greater amounts of cash provides them with more freedom to spend and save as they please. Volunteer opportunities, which can introduce young people to the broader concept of community responsibility, also become available at this age.

Teenagers begin spending less time at home and more time with their friends. However, as the peer group takes on ever-greater importance, adolescents often settle into a funk when they are at home. This is the age when many parents complain that their child has become a stranger, unwilling to talk about his activities, distant from his siblings, and scornful of once-cherished family rituals. While parental supervision remains vital—perhaps more vital than ever in helping teens use good judgment—it must be handled with great tact, as adolescents bristle at any hint that their privacy is being invaded or that their autonomy or judgment are being questioned.

As adolescents are exposed to the temptations of a larger world, they begin to think more deeply about what is right and wrong and to exercise their own sense of judgment. Most likely cigarettes, alcohol, or drugs will cross their paths for the first time. Peers may challenge them to engage in a variety of risk-taking behaviors. While an emerging independent ethical sense is a tremendously exciting thing for a parent to witness, this is also the age at which its absence can spawn great tragedy. Here is where loving support without undue control from parents can be so important in reinforcing their child's self-esteem and affirming their confidence in him, which will enable him to resist dangerous pressure. By allowing teens to rebel in safer areas, such as with clothes and hairstyles, parents then can be firmer in expecting responsible behavior regarding large issues, such as drugs.

By the time children reach the often-dreaded teen years, parents may see unexpected positive results in their efforts to instill responsibility and a caring attitude. Just when things seem to be toughest, a teenager may suddenly let his parents know how much he loves them and how much he appreciates their continued guidance and support. Raising a child to become a responsible adult is not an easy job, but there are rewards along the way that make the effort eminently worthwhile.

• • • • • • • • • • • • • • • • • • • • • • • • • • • • • • • • • • •

## Parents ask:

*For the fourth time this year, my eight-year-old son lost his book bag. I've tried everything from punishing him to pinning a note to his jacket to remind him to check for it before he leaves school, the bus, or the playground. Nothing has worked. Is he always going to be so irresponsible?*

Most kids do not continually lose something just to be bad or irresponsible. While it's upsetting (and costly) and extremely frustrating, there's often more to losing a book bag than meets the eye. Beside general forgetfulness, a child may have trouble keeping the connection in his mind between what he's told to do and actually doing it in his everyday life, or he may be having trouble with his class, a teacher, or friends. In a small number of cases, he may have a learning problem. By talking with her son, this parent may be able to discover any negative feelings he has about school or a teacher. A learning problem may be indicated by clumsiness, illegible handwriting, or poor spelling. If there is no learning or school difficulty, the mother can approach the problem in many ways. She can write to or speak personally with the teacher or a teacher's aide to enlist help in checking the book bag to make sure her son is carrying the minimum possible load, as well as to remind him to take it home and not lose it. As an alternative, she could enlist the help of one of her son's friends to remind him. She also could use a point system in which she rewards her son with special privileges when he doesn't lose the bag. Most important, since this is a phase that usually passes, she can buy inexpensive book bags!

# CHAPTER TWO

......

# What Is a Parent's Role?

**M**ost parents view the birth of a child, especially the first child, with a complex mixture of joy and apprehension. From the moment the baby is brought home, the parents are faced with the awesome responsibility of guiding a seemingly helpless infant through the years toward becoming a responsible adult.

In the past, the infant mind was viewed as an empty slate waiting to be filled. The newborn also was seen as a small savage in need of training in how to control her impulses. The parents' role was to teach proper behavior and provide the child with incentives for being good. More recent research in child development, however, has revealed that even in the earliest stages of life children are sensitive to those around them and feel connected to their environment. Infants appear able to empathize with others and choose how connected or withdrawn they want to be. This early awareness suggests that a desire for a mutually satisfying parent-child relationship is intact and complete in every newborn.

This new understanding points to a natural approach toward raising responsible children. Rather than being unapproachable teachers of responsibility, parents can view themselves as the vital link between their children and the world. By providing a safe, responsive, nurturing environment, especially during the critical first year, parents lay a groundwork of trust that they will build on as their child grows. The environment parents should create requires staying attuned to the infinite variety of signals coming from their baby and responding with loving touches and cuddles; words; smiles and funny faces; and by providing opportunities for exploring the world, as well as supplying the basic needs of food and comfort. As developmental psychologist Thomas Lickona, Ph.D., says in his book, *Raising Good Children*, ''That first attachment, that human bond, is the indispensable basis for later moral development.''

As children grow, parents can take advantage of their child's continuing desire to please by letting her know again and again that responsible behavior pleases caring adults. Along the way, the parents' continuing role is to remain aware of their child's level of moral development and to tailor their expectations accordingly; provide age-appropriate challenges that encourage moral development; define and enforce appropriate rules and limits; serve as a role model; and communicate through listening, questioning, praise, and helpful criticism.

Such a role may sound relatively easy to accomplish. After all, parents love their children and want to do all they can to help their children grow up to be good people. However, most parents know they have their own limitations, just as their children do. As they learn and grow with their children, parents can expect to make mistakes at times. It's not easy to know when to protect a child and when to let go, when to intervene and when to allow her to suffer the consequences of her own misjudgments. Nor can parents expect to be considerate at every moment or serve as an ideal role model for their children at all times.

Fortunately, children are resilient and won't be shattered by occasional judgment lapses or a flash of parental bad temper. Just as parents try to teach their children to learn from mistakes, parents also must learn from their own mistakes—and learn not to judge themselves too harshly. When a parent finds herself angry with her children, for instance, she needs to remember to stop and think why she is upset. Are the children truly misbehaving, or is she having a bad day for whatever reasons? Once she knows why she is upset, she can communicate in a way her children will understand. For example, she could say to her school-age children, "I'm sorry I yelled at you, but I'm very tired. If you can't play quietly for awhile, you will have to go to your room. We can play a game together a little later." If a parent's reaction is inappropriately strong, she still can forgive herself for the mistake and work to do better next time. By doing so, she will be teaching her children to do the same.

## The Art of Modeling

Children are careful observers of the world around them and learn their earliest lessons by watching adults, especially their parents. This means that children are just as likely to imitate bad models as they are to follow good ones.

To illustrate the importance of modeling, parents might try thinking back to when they were children or teenagers and remembering what a parent or other adult may have said or done that helped them learn what it means to be a responsible person. On the positive side, one mother remembers, "My father was very firm about throwing papers and trash in the proper place. Sometimes we carried paper cups or gum wrappers for blocks before we found a trash can we could put them in. He asked me to think what it would be like if everyone littered. That thought helped me remember to this day how important my own actions are." On the negative side, a father remembers,

"When I first got my driver's license, my mother lectured me on driving safely and following traffic laws. However, *she* rarely stayed within speed limits when she drove. She got away with it, so I could see no reason why I shouldn't be able to."

By remembering how their parents and other adults influenced them when they were young and what kind of adults they would like their own children to be, parents can think about the kinds of behavior they would like to model. One mother explained her thinking: "I talk about my values and why they work for me and why they are important to me. I try very hard to 'practice what I preach.' I tell my children it is wrong to lie, and I try very hard not to lie myself. This includes little white lies as well. I wouldn't want to attempt to explain to my five-year-old son why I just told someone on the phone that Daddy isn't home when Daddy is sitting in the living room watching television."

Some of the traits children can learn from parental example include:

- A willingness to admit mistakes
- An ability to talk openly about feelings and to communicate needs
- Tolerance for differences among people
- Empathy for other people
- Respect for agreed-upon rules and laws
- Willingness to stand up for values
- Dependability and punctuality
- The value of participation in community activities
- Honesty in dealing with other people
- The determination to overcome obstacles
- The value of generosity with no expected return
- The importance of learning
- Sportsmanship

While it is always worthwhile to talk about responsibility and ethical behavior to children, a parent's example can be more persuasive. The old adage ''Actions speak louder than words'' holds true, as evidenced by the father's earlier quote about his mother's driving. Parents need to be aware of what messages they may be sending by their actions and body language as well as through their words. If parents preach one action, such as the value of being a contributing member of the community, and then never volunteer for anything (such as chaperoning a school group) or never bother to vote, attend a town meeting, join a church or block committee, address envelopes for a political candidate, or even attend a local parade, their children are unlikely to take their words seriously and will come to think of them as hypocrites.

Modeling responsibility through words and actions can take place with almost any activity that parents and children share. For example, babies can see how to treat a pet by watching a parent properly play with and care for an animal. Two-year-olds benefit from watching and then copying an action with a parent, such as putting toys away in a toy box or books on a shelf. Four-year-olds can be encouraged to choose an old but serviceable toy to give to charity while a parent collects his own old clothes to give away. Children will also understand the benefits of generous behavior when parents express in words and by general attitude that giving to others makes them feel good. School-age children may take more of an interest in reading if they see that their parents regularly enjoy reading for pleasure. They also will benefit from other good role models, such as teachers. Preteens will understand the value of a good reputation and how it is affected by their actions. A parent who finishes projects she starts and who encourages her children to do the same will also be modeling patience and determination. An example of a good model for teenagers who may be tempted to smoke, drink, or experiment with drugs is a parent who quits smoking and expresses the value of quitting while admitting how difficult it is.

Being a good role model at all times is not possible for most parents, but they can do their best by stopping now and then to consider how their words might sound or their actions might look to their children. If the model is not what parents want to portray, they can vow to try harder and still guide their children by explaining why sometimes they are not good examples, thereby showing their children that parents are human, too.

## The Journey Toward Independence

The growth from infancy to young adulthood is continually marked by new responsibilities. A wise parent, wrote psychologist Haim G. Ginott, Ph.D., in *Between Parent and Child,* is one who makes herself increasingly *dispensable* to children. From the day a child ties her own shoes to the first time she gets behind the wheel of a car, she relishes the right to say, "I did it myself." The parent's role is to offer appropriate praise and encouragement for accomplishments and honest effort alike and to recognize the child's need for independence. "The goal of fostering a child's development toward independence embodies more than teaching a child to drink out of a cup or to dress himself," writes Elaine Heffner, Ed. D., in *Mothering.* "The goal is to nurture the development of autonomy, the capacity for independent thinking, for problem solving, the unique attributes of an individual personality."

## Is She Ready?

Determining when a child is ready to assume greater control over her life is no easy task. When she is six, her parents may have to decide whether or not she can ride her bicycle around the block without supervision; at 13 or 14, the pressing question is more likely whether or not she can date outside of a group or without a chaperone. At every stage, decisions require a reasonable balance between the need to protect children from physical and emotional harm and the value of giving them new responsibilities and new opportunities to learn.

An almost universal truth about most children of any age is that their reach often exceeds their grasp. Whether the issue is how high to climb a tree or how late to stay out with friends, children strain to go further and faster, to do and see more, to pry open life's secrets, and, as it sometimes seems to the adults around them, to grow up as quickly as possible. Every parent of a youngster old enough to talk is familiar with the way a child bargains, cajoles, makes comparisons, and asks for exceptions in order to do more. ("Jesse gets to stay up until 10 P.M., why can't I?" "Don't help me put the puzzle together. I want to do it by myself." "Please let me ride my bike alone now. I promise to be careful.")

Although the subjects of dispute change as children become adolescents, the basic themes remain much the same. ("Why can't I go to the party? Erin's parents will be just down the block and all the other kids are going." "Why can't I bleach my hair? I'm the only girl in class who doesn't do it.")

How do parents know when their children are ready for new responsibilities or more independence? How do they know when to let children try more, to hold them back, or to give a little push forward? Clues to children's readiness to tackle new challenges and take on new responsibilities come from careful observation of their behavior and from hints in what they say. Parents can begin by looking at what a child is already able to do. If a six- or seven-year-old can carefully sort and stack a card collection, then she might be ready to take responsibility for organizing her own school books on the shelves in her room or to help a parent organize closets and drawers. It could also mean that she's ready for more privileges, such as being given greater freedom in choosing her own clothes.

Clues to fears about taking on new responsibilities may come from what a child *doesn't* say or do as much as from what she *does*. For example, a teenager who refuses to talk about her distress about entering high school may decide on her own to seek her parents' advice once she realizes that they know that her fears are normal, not silly or childish.

While attempting to read the often mixed signals from their children, parents must try to maintain a delicate balance between giving constructive guidance and rules that either provide a child with more autonomy than she can handle or squash her developmental progress. For some kids, an explanation or introduction to a new responsibility is all they need. Other children require more guidance or need more time to develop the maturity or skills to take on additional responsibility. All children, however, need parents who will create the necessary scaffolding for responsible behavior. Younger children who are learning to put away blocks may need their parents to set up storage space and then help them share the chore. This groundwork gives children support for successfully completing the task. For older children, the scaffolding may be more theoretical. In teaching a child how to handle money independently, for example, a parent might provide a frame of reference for how much the child can spend on personal wants by helping her outline a weekly or monthly budget.

Another way for parents to determine readiness for new responsibilities is to let children prove they can handle a new task or make a wise decision in the parents' presence before being permitted to do so alone. Sometimes some follow-up may be needed. One mother, for example, explained to her seven-year-old son what she expected if she were to allow him to ride his bicycle without adult supervision. She added, "I'll surprise you and follow you sometimes." Despite her warning, she reports, "I didn't like what he did; he didn't follow my instructions. So he won't be allowed to ride his bicycle alone for a while." Other parents will find themselves pleasantly surprised by their child's mature behavior.

Once parents decide that their child is ready to try something new, they can communicate their confidence by saying such things as "Now that you are getting older, you are ready to do more things" and "I know that you are careful about crossing the street, so you can go over to Corey's house by yourself now." A child also can be prepared for a new adventure by comparing it to a familiar event or a past success: "You've spent a lot of time at Grandma's house, so I know you'll enjoy spending the night. You can choose some of your favorite toys and books to take with you." If the child is fearful of a new stage of development, more than an expression of confidence may be needed, such as understanding ("I know you are scared") and reassurance of how a parent will help ("You can call me from Grandma's house"). When *parents* are the ones who are fearful, they may say, "I know you are ready, but since I am a little nervous, please call me from Grandma's."

Introducing new responsibilities is initially very time-consuming for parents. In the short run, for instance, it often seems easier to dress a child than to wait three times as long for her to dress herself and then see her emerge from her room with all the clothes on backwards. In situations such as this, a parent may need to lay out the clothes the night before and talk about what will take place the next morning, start the morning 20 minutes earlier, and take the time to supervise the dressing at first, spending less time as the child demonstrates proficiency.

A good approach is for parents to start teaching new skills when they don't feel rushed or impatient. They should look at their daily schedule and see where there might be some flexibility to build in more time or where teaching can be included with activities that are already on the schedule. One mother of two preschoolers says, "I've tried to bring my chores to their level, such as chopping vegetables near them and letting them touch, taste, and help with a similar and safer tool; putting up a small clothesline where they can hang up their clothes; letting them sort their clothes after they've been washed; and pulling a chair up to the sink to let them clean vegetables and wash unbreakable dishes."

Not every attempt to insert responsibility into an already hectic schedule will work the first time. In the face of time pressures and threatened chaos, parents may have to take charge and do the job alone, decide to leave it half finished, or push and help a child do what's necessary. The important thing is to keep trying. It can be frustrating, but in the long run the effort pays off. One mother of three, who had made a point of teaching her older children to take a reasonable amount of responsibility, related the following story:

*One day my five-year-old could see that I was really upset that the baby was taking so much time and I had not done the laundry or started dinner. When Jaclyn was finally asleep, I returned to the living room and found that Gina had taken all the laundry out of the dryer and had folded it all, and that Lori (age 3) was carrying the folded laundry back to the basket. I was really touched, since I had not asked for that help. At that point it didn't even matter that the basement had toys from one end to the other that they had not cleaned up.*

Parents also need to make sure that new decision-making opportunities are closely matched with their children's particular stage of development. For example, a three-year-old child cannot be expected to select all of her clothes. Ask her what she wants to wear and she will most likely select the outfit that appeals to her at the moment: shorts in the winter perhaps, or a snowsuit in July. To encourage a sense of autonomy without allowing her to select clothing that is entirely inappropriate to the season, a parent can instead ask a child to select from a range of options. ("Donna, do you want to wear your red shirt today or the blue one?" "Here are three pairs of socks that match your outfit. Which ones do you want to wear?".)

Food is another common dilemma. Ask a young child what she wants for breakfast and parents are more likely to get a request for ice cream or candy than for a bowl of nourishing cereal. But giving her a choice between cereal or toast demonstrates respect for her personal preferences while ensuring that she has a healthful meal.

Applying these principles increasingly grows more challenging as children grow older and become capable of doing more. For example, eight-year-old Jennifer is proud that she is allowed to choose what she wears to school, but if her parents don't approve of her choice—such as a pink plaid top with a green striped skirt—a conflict may result. Although her parents should feel free to express their opinion, they should not disparage Jennifer's choice. Otherwise they might be sending the message "It is fine to make your own decisions about clothes so long as we agree with your choice." In general, if no harm is likely to come from a child's decision, as in the case of Jennifer's wild-patterned outfit, it is best to respect her choices and allow her to learn from them.

By the time children reach the teenage years, parents expect them to make even more of their own decisions. Indeed, most young adults insist on it. If they have had practice making their own decisions all along, teens will be better able to make wise decisions in situations with more serious consequences at stake.

## Please Set Limits for Me

While children's enthusiasm for new experiences can be infectious, their fearlessness can be alarming. In the interest of safety, parents need to determine just how far their children's grasp actually extends. Beginning at the toddler stage and continuing through the teenage years, setting age-appropriate limits that match a child's capabilities becomes one of the most challenging tasks of parenting.

Even though children can be expected to push constantly against these limits, they are privately relieved to have them enforced. Child development expert T. Berry Brazelton, M.D., author of *Toddlers and Parents: A Declaration of Independence*, shows great insight in writing of the toddler: "His new-found freedom is fraught with danger, and a child this age recognizes it. He demonstrates his awareness of the danger every time he goes toward a prohibited place, by turning back with a wicked gleam in his eye, fairly pleading for a parental 'no.' " Although the dynamics differ somewhat, older children are equally daring and equally dependent on restrictions set by their parents. While balking at curfews or protesting a request to call home during an evening out, a teenager is relieved of the anxiety of too much responsibility by reasonable restrictions. The following two stories illustrate this principle.

*Eight-year-old Zachary loves to play in the ocean waves and is a secure and competent swimmer. Zachary's mother points out the boundaries beyond which he cannot swim, then watches from the water's edge. At first Zachary stays close to shore; then he gradually swims farther away until he is beyond the set limit. When his mother calls him back, he swims quickly into the agreed-upon boundaries, looking relieved.*

*Fifteen-year-old Alexandria asks to stay out past her curfew in order to join a group of older teens for a midnight barbecue and pool party. When her father reminds her of what the rules are, she complains that he treats her like a baby, becomes angry, and stomps away in a huff. Her father later overhears her tell a friend on the telephone, ''I really want to go, but my dad said he'd ground me for a month if I do.*

Although their situations are different, Zachary and Alexandria both wanted to have limits established and enforced for them. Zachary was waiting for someone to notice that he'd strayed too far, while Alexandria may have felt uncomfortable with the party invitation but needed the exaggerated excuse of her father's strictness to turn it down. Probably neither of them would admit to this. Nonetheless, their sense of security depended heavily on the knowledge that someone was there to draw a line beyond which they were not permitted to cross.

With this in mind, parents should not be afraid to say no. However, a rule that is continually challenged may signal that parents and children need to talk it over and work out a solution together. The rule may not fit the specific temperament and abilities of the child. For example, instead of enforcing a time for going to bed, a parent may allow a teenager to set her own bedtime if she can demonstrate that less sleep will not injure her health or prevent her from meeting her responsibilities in school. Limits also may be easier to enforce if children are allowed to rebel occasionally and express their independence in "safer" areas, such as choosing clothes and hairstyles. They may then be more willing to accept parental authority in other areas, such as keeping up with schoolwork and observing curfew times.

Children will also be more cooperative in accepting limits if parents explain the reasons behind the rules and demonstrate that the restrictions they impose are based on love. Most children generally don't think rules are bad, especially if the rules are justified. In their book *Bringing Up a Moral Child*, psychologists Michael Schulman, Ph.D., and Eva Mekler write, "When parents make clear statements of reasons, a child learns that they care about his intentions as well as his actions. . . . Teaching reasons sets the framework for the transfer of power over the child's behavior from the parents to the child." Of course, no parent wants to explain every rule every time it's enforced. However, by trying to establish an early habit of *briefly* explaining their reasoning, parents remind their child that they care about her, respect her, and would be willing to discuss a change in the rule if she is ready to move forward. Since many children do not seem to listen the first several times something is explained, parents need to remember that it's important to keep trying.

## Two Steps Forward, One Step Back

Children who are stretching into new territory are likely to be excited about the challenges ahead. Anxiety, however, usually, accompanies independence, making them feel vulnerable and badly in need of reassurance and support.

Children's regression into irresponsible behavior after showing that they are capable of handling responsibility may be easier for parents to tolerate if they remember that progress cannot be marked by a perfectly straight upward line. Children do not take on ever greater responsibilities until total independence is achieved. Instead, the process is somewhat cyclical. The same child who insists on dressing herself and who shows that she can do so with great confidence may suddenly revert to infantile behavior that appears to be deliberately defiant. Actually, the child is just demonstrating a very human insecurity: Having gone so far out on a limb of self-reliance, she suddenly senses that she is at risk and needs to be reassured that her parents are still there to keep her safe and to care about her. In *Mothering*, summing up the conflicting influences that act on children of any age, Dr. Elaine Heffner writes, "The counterpressure of the push to independence is the pull back to dependence."

This push-pull progress toward independence may be demonstrated by a three-year-old who suddenly wants a bottle and reverts to baby talk after the arrival of a new baby brother. A six-year-old child who is old enough to play alone with her friends in the neighborhood may still run into the house occasionally for her mother's reassuring touch. Adolescents often look to their parents for much the same protection, although they are generally reluctant to admit it. A teenager may hover silently nearby while a parent is cooking. She may have something on her mind, or she may simply want the comfort of being near Mom or Dad. Another child may be a veteran member of the school band, but she still seeks the reassurance and encouragement from her parents' presence in the audience and their show of pride.

## Building a Child's Self-Esteem

One of a parent's most important responsibilities is to help children build self-esteem, which is truly a springboard into a rewarding life. Building self-esteem means providing a child with both roots and wings. The roots provide a sense of belonging and security, while the wings encourage her to venture into the world independently, with confidence, curiosity, and a strong sense of self.

Research shows that when a child is confident of her parents' unconditional love, she cares about herself and in turn is able to care about others. As Matthew Fox, an educator, writes in *Original Blessing*, ''Healthy families remind each other of their goodness; unhealthy families remind each other of their failings.'' From infancy on, parents can solidify a child's self-worth by reminding her of her goodness and letting her know they are glad she is their child. The following are some additional thoughts to consider that enhance a child's self-image:

- **Value children for themselves, not for what they accomplish.** This may mean saying to a child now and then, ''You're really a great person to be with,'' instead of saving praise just for achievements such as good grades or cleaning up a room. Parents will know they have succeeded in enhancing a child's self-image when a child responds to an out-of-the-blue hug with a comment such as ''What's that for?'' ''Just because I felt like hugging you,'' a parent may reply.
- **Respect children's individuality rather than imposing unfulfilled parental dreams upon them.** A school-age child may not be much interested in or very skillful at art, even though her father showed great but unrealized promise as an artist when he was young. However, the

42

child may show mechanical ability and would love more encouragement and opportunities to develop this talent.

- **Listen to children and take their concerns seriously.** This means setting aside time to talk with a child, away from other distractions. It also means listening without interrupting, making comments that acknowledge her feelings, and asking questions that help her reach her own solution. For example, a teenager may be nervous about giving a report in class or going to a school dance, or may be upset by a friend's cruel treatment of someone else. Instead of just telling the child not to worry or not to get involved, a parent can help her think about her feelings and evaluate options. Parents will know their listening has been successful when children come up with more questions than parents are asking. The balance then shifts from a one-sided parental lecture to real communication.

- **Set reasonable expectations and be tolerant of mistakes and foibles.** This includes making sure a child understands a rule before expecting her to follow it and that she knows how to do something before expecting her to do it. Parents should remember that everyone starts at the beginning and needs time to practice and to learn from mistakes. Children also need encouragement to keep trying; they need praise for their efforts as well as for their accomplishments. Expectations should also be age-appropriate. For example, if a seven-year-old constantly forgets to bring home schoolwork or loses track of her possessions, perhaps she needs help in organizing things as well as developing ideas for self-reminders. Children usually do not want to repeat a mistake, so parents may know that a task is beyond their child's capabilities when the problem occurs more than one or two times.

- **Create a foundation of trust from which children feel it**

**is safe to venture forth.** Avoid ridicule or condemnation, including name-calling. To be told that something a child *did* was unwise is quite different from being told that she *herself* is stupid. Children who trust their parents to be encouraging and understanding are more willing to try new things and to discuss their experiences. This encouragement can be exhibited even when parents are amused by their children's first attempts at a new adult behavior. Often the parents recognize and remember their own trials while growing up. Parents should just be sure to communicate that they are laughing at their memories of themselves, not at the child.

- **Whenever possible, entrust children with making their own decisions.** By doing so, they will learn to trust their own judgment. These decisions also must be age-appropriate and linked to situations where the decision will not endanger or harm the child or another person. For example, a toddler can choose what to eat for lunch, but she should not be allowed to choose whether or not to wear her car seat belt.

- **Whenever possible, provide opportunities for children to stretch toward new heights.** These opportunities can be quite simple, such as entrusting a five-year-old with store coupons and the job of matching the pictures on the coupons to the products on the shelves. Whatever ''stretching exercises'' you offer, be sure that they are tailored to a child's capabilities in order to avoid frustration.

- **Assume the best and give credit for good intentions.** Children who know that their parents understand that they are trying to do their best will keep trying. They also will be more tolerant of their own mistakes, which will in time extend to a tolerance for other people's best efforts, even if those efforts do not completely succeed.

Opportunities for building children's self-esteem are readily available. As one mother of a seven-year-old girl said, "You pick out the thing in your child that you think is terrific and tell her about it. Don't miss it. My daughter has a friend who is a terrific speller. My daughter said, 'That's what Valerie is good at. What am I good at?' I told her, 'You're good at cartwheels.' She was apparently so pleased with my remark that she spent the rest of the evening doing cartwheels."

Be alert to opportunities that might get lost in a moment of thoughtlessness, as in the following example of a father watching his son's performance in a soccer game: The father cheered his son from the sidelines. When the boy missed a shot, his dad was about to scream, "Hey, what do you think you're doing?" But he remembered an earlier, anguished look that had crossed his son's face when he had made an error. Instead, the father called, "Good try, son. Hang in there!" When the team lost, this father reminded his son that he would have another chance next month to play the winning team. As a result of his father's encouragement, the boy felt he had done his best and acknowledged that the game was fun even though his team lost.

These parental messages have great impact, often becoming self-fulfilling prophecies that affect a child's behavior well into adulthood. When parents communicate confidence, trust, and pride, children learn that their parents expect them to succeed and assume that they will. Conversely, when a parent constantly expresses doubt about a child's capabilities, that child may say to herself, "My parents expect me to fail, and they are probably right."

# Praise and Criticism:
# The Art of Providing Feedback

An important rule of thumb that most parents know but may sometimes forget in the hectic pace of daily life is to "praise more than you punish." A child should not have to misbehave to receive attention. Parents who always criticize poor behavior and seldom offer praise cause their children to conclude, in effect, "No one notices when I'm being good. If I am going to make Mom and Dad pay attention to me, I will have to make them angry."

As Dr. Haim G. Ginott wrote in *Between Parent and Child,* "There is no escape from the fact that a child learns what he lives. If he lives with criticism, he does not learn responsibility. He learns to condemn himself and to find fault with others. He learns to doubt his own judgment, to disparage his own ability, and to distrust the intentions of others. And above all, he learns to live with continual expectation of impending doom."

To counter too-frequent criticisms, parents can let their child know that they notice when she is in good spirits and behaving well. When she offers to share toys with her friends, asks for something politely, or helps around the house before being asked, parents can make a point of telling her how much they appreciate her thoughtfulness. The following are some examples of positive feedback parents can offer:

> "That was very generous of you to let Donald play with your favorite truck. I'm sure you made him happy."
> "Thanks for letting me know ahead of time that you needed a snack for your class trip. That gave me time to plan instead of having to rush at the last minute."
> "Thanks for taking out the garbage. That helps me out."

"I trust you to keep your word because you understand how much we value integrity in this family."

In the long run, parental affirmation is more effective in building character than is constant nagging and criticism. On the other hand, it is important to give praise only when it is deserved and not to overpraise in order to win a child's affections. Children have an instinct for discerning phoniness and may resent being praised when they don't think it is deserved. Furthermore, halfhearted efforts that win praise from parents are not going to be appreciated by others with whom a child interacts.

Parents may be able to stop their tendency to criticize by first trying to think about why a child has acted inappropriately. It may be because the child doesn't know how to think a case through. In such a situation, a parent could help a child work through her own reasoning. For example, Ellen's five-year-old daughter kept forgetting to close the gate to the house. Instead of continuing to yell at her, Ellen sat down with her daughter and talked about what might happen as a result of carelessness. "What could happen if you leave the gate open?" asked Ellen. After some thought, her daughter answered, "The twins [who are 18 months old] could walk out in the street. Or a big dog could come into our yard." Once Ellen recognized these possible dangers, it was easy for her to understand when her mom said, "Let's be sure to keep the gate closed and locked from now on, okay?" (Keep in mind, however, that while it's important for Ellen to see to it that the gate is closed, it's too much to ask a five-year-old to be in charge of her siblings' safety.)

When unacceptable behavior calls for sterner measures, parental disapproval still should focus on the act itself, and not on the child's character. Rather than call a child clumsy when she spills milk at dinner, remind her to think about where she is reaching next time and have her help you clean it up. If a child is hostile and disruptive at the dinner table, try not to campaign against him as a human being. Generalized statements such as, "You are so unpleasant, you ruin every meal," are counterproductive. If a child is out of control, a more effective way to bring peace might be to say, "I can't enjoy my dinner with all this racket. Please go to your room. Feel free to join us again when you are calmer."

Here are some other examples of statements that express a personal reaction to a child's *behavior*, rather than judgments that often tend to generalize and condemn:

"I get upset when you promise to clean your room and then don't follow through on your promise" (instead of "You're a slob!").

"I'm worried about your attitude toward your sister. Why do you always pinch her when you know it makes her cry?" (instead of "You're mean!").

"I'm tired when I get home from work, and I just can't handle seeing the kitchen in such a mess" (instead of "Why are you so lazy?").

Trying to tailor criticism to the situation is hard for any parent, especially when the adult may be angry because she feels she is not getting through to her child, frustrated at having to deal with the same inappropriate behavior again and again, or reminded of something in herself or another person that she doesn't like. The important thing for a parent to remember is to keep trying, and to apologize for calling a child names if it does occur. When parents feel that much of their relationship with a child seems negative, it may also help to look for ways to spend time with her when the situation doesn't call for trying to manage or control her behavior. Even time spent reading together can provide an enjoyable break from the "Do this, don't do that" routine.

## Establish Explicit Rules

One way to reduce conflict and criticism is to establish explicit household rules *before* conflict arises. This also has the beneficial effect of reducing children's feelings that they are being unfairly treated. When children also have input into rulemaking and believe that rules are established with their best interests in mind, they are more likely to comply with parental guidelines.

Here are some ways to establish fair and effective rules at home:

- **Talk with children about why rules are necessary.** Parents might mention the need for everyone to cooperate to keep the household running smoothly, the importance of assuring everyone's safety, and their wish to help children learn responsibility.
- **Ask children for input into rules while still limiting choices.** For example, rather than ask "How much television do you think you should watch?" parents might ask, "Would you prefer to watch an hour of television before your homework is completed, or afterwards?"
- **Be certain that any household rules are clear and consistent and that children understand them.**
- **Don't permit many exceptions to established rules.** Sometimes a child's sheer persistence tempts parents to bend just to gain some peace and quiet, but this only teaches a child that badgering pays off. If a child honestly feels that a rule needs to be changed because she is ready for more responsibility, parents can permit a trial period to allow her a chance to show her readiness.
- **Emphasize Consequences.** When a child breaks rules,

**49**

parents need to make sure that she understands how other people are affected by her actions. Helping a child to mop up a mess on the kitchen floor while explaining that this is a preventive measure so that no one slips and gets hurt is more effective than complaining that the child is sloppy or clumsy.

- **Parents and children can agree in advance on appropriate disciplinary measures when the rules are disobeyed.** Then be sure that the punishment fits the act and the age. For example, a five-minute time-out for throwing sand at the playground makes a big impression on a two-year-old. A summer weekend without the company of friends can be adequate punishment for an eight-year-old who neglected to tell her parents that she suddenly decided to visit a friend five blocks away. (For more information about effective discipline, read the Children's Television Workshop's *Parents' Guide to Understanding Discipline*.)

## Living with Consequences

As children begin to make more of their own decisions, they inevitably make some mistakes. Allowing a child to learn from the consequences of a bad decision is seldom easy for a loving parent. Such a parent is tempted to intervene to spare the child unhappiness or just to bring peace to the family. While protecting a child from physical injury is always appropriate, sheltering her from embarrassing, irritating, or inconvenient consequences of an error or reneging on the enforcement of consequences is, of course, abdicating a parent's own responsibility.

"We can't always protect and defend our children," says one mother of a 12-year-old daughter and a nine-year-old son. "There's nothing wrong with them realizing that life is not always going to be easy. I think we do our children a disservice by caving in to spare them any discomfort." Although it is hard to stand by and watch children in emotional pain (whether it is because they didn't make the track team or win the spelling bee, or because a favorite toy is lost as a result of carelessness, or because they can't go to a party after breaking a rule), the discovery that life can be disappointing is a lesson that everyone must learn. Even toddlers can learn that if they mishandle a toy it can break and that it won't be instantly replaced.

At a young age, when the consequences of most decisions are relatively mild, children can learn that choices must be carefully considered because the results cannot always be readily reversed. Two parents give examples of these early decisions:

*We had gone to our summer cottage at the end of May, and the lake was still very cold. I didn't think it a good idea for Megen to swim or wade, but I kept my mouth closed and let her decide. She made it up to her knees and was extremely cold. Out she came, asking, "When do you think it will be warm enough to swim?" There were no more requests to go in the water over the weekend.*

*Our dog has proven to be a wonderful teacher to my eight-year-old son in terms of helping him learn to keep toys off his floor. His room used to be dangerous to enter, but since we got our dog, and the dog chewed up some dominoes and cars, my son keeps the floor entirely clear!*

By sometime later in life, when decisions have more significant ramifications, the groundwork for making wise choices will have been laid. If parents are always rescuing the erring child—carrying forgotten lunch boxes to school, purchasing new toys when old ones are carelessly broken, giving constant reminders about doing homework or chores (or even doing the homework themselves), and explaining away irresponsible behavior toward a child's friends or teachers—their children may grow up believing that there will always be someone to get them out of hot water. As adults, of course, they have to face harsher truths, and the consequences of poor judgment are invariably more severe.

Here are some suggestions adapted from Nancy Samalin and Martha Moraghan Jablow's book *Loving Your Child Is Not Enough* that might help parents reduce overprotectiveness beyond the requirements of safety or empathy:

- **Children need to learn to do things their way, even though parents may feel embarrassed or helpless when children suffer the consequences.** For example, if a child who had agreed to be in charge of buying a birthday present for a friend's party forgets to do so, parents can't worry that this oversight reflects on them as parents. Nor should they rush in to save their child from the feelings of embarrassment that are natural under the circumstances.
- **If a child is having a hard time with something, such as making friends in school or getting along with a teacher, parents should try not to blame the situation on themselves or rush in to fix it.** However, they can be empathetic and try to help their child sort out her feelings and work toward a solution.
- **Once children have demonstrated that they can take care of themselves, give them credit for doing so.** If parents think their child will be cold if she doesn't wear a jacket, they may mention it. But if in her rush to go somewhere she refuses to wear one, she may have to experience what it's like to be cold.
- **Encourage children to take charge of the parts of their**

**life that they can handle.** For example, if a preteen wants to reschedule a piano lesson in order to attend a baseball game, she can call her piano teacher herself.

- **Parents can remind themselves that they should do less, not more, for their children as they grow.** However, guidance will always be needed until a child has reached adulthood.

## "I Know How You Feel"

As explained earlier, the capacity to empathize with others or to understand another's viewpoint is an important component of responsibility. Parents can support the growth of their child's sense of compassion by showing empathy for her, by encouraging her to think about other people's feelings, and by showing that small acts of kindness can make a difference.

It is never too early or too late to inculcate this trait. Keep in mind, however, that empathy shows itself differently in each child, and the same child can exhibit empathy differently at different ages. Boys and girls also tend to differ in the style of their empathic responses. According to psychologist Carol Gilligan, Ph.D., these differences occur because boys and girls identify differently with women, who are still the primary caretakers of most children. Girls grow up with a connectedness and a knowledge of their similarity to their mothers, whereas boys grow up with an awareness of their differences. As a result, girls move more easily toward caring and responsibility for others that they see demonstrated by their mothers. In general, boys may need more coaching to think about other people's feelings, while girls may need guidance in curbing their tendency to give too much at the expense of their own needs. The following are some examples of what parents may do to foster empathy in children of various ages:

**A three-year-old child can be reminded that other people know and care about what she does.** A parent can say, "When you help me, I feel good" or "Here's a chance to do something nice for your friend and make her happy." By the age of four, most children are aware that other people have viewpoints, but they usually aren't able to consider them. If parents make an effort to present another's viewpoint, however, their child is likely to understand, especially if it is presented in terms of what's fair. Parents may say to a child that it's not fair to parents to leave toys around where they can be stepped on. Parents also may be rewarded by early flashes of empathy from children, who at this age seem naturally generous.

**Five-year-olds can respond to such questions as "How would you feel if someone wouldn't play with you?" or "Why do you think Grandma got angry?"** This reminds them to consider the emotional realities of other people. When a neighbor's husband died, one mother sat down with her five-year-old son to talk about how sad the neighbor was feeling. Later, at her son's initiative, they bought the woman a flowering bush and planted it for her.

**Six- and seven-year-olds and even older children may benefit from role-playing to help them imagine being in someone else's shoes.** For example, with a child who steals something from another child, parents might role-play a situation in which a favorite toy is taken away. Then they can talk about how it felt to have something stolen. Parents might also appeal to a child's sense of fairness and encourage empathy by saying "I did something nice for you; now you do something nice for me." Be careful, however, not to overuse this tactic since, after all, parents are *supposed* to be nice to their kids and kids should not come to feel that parental kindness has strings attached.

**As children approach the age of nine or 10, they can understand the concept of doing something nice for someone out of love without expecting something in return.** To help a child identify with someone else's emotional response, she might be reminded of how she could help the person ("Remember how unhappy you felt when the kids teased you about your braces and how happy you were about your straight teeth when the braces finally came off last year? Maybe you could tell your little sister about that experience so she won't feel so bad about getting braces").

**Older children are also capable of putting themselves in someone else's shoes.** If you witness your son excluding another child from his game, for example, you could say, "Gregory must be very upset because you wouldn't let him play kickball. Imagine how badly you would feel if the boys kept you off the team."

Preteens and teenagers can be encouraged to think about the feelings of people whom they have never met. This can lead to discussions on the effects of prejudice and discrimination. They also can follow through on the effects one person's actions may have on a group of people, both positively and negatively. They can learn to enjoy exercising compassion for others even when they aren't able to see immediate results, such as collecting food for the homeless or toys for needy children. They are able to care about other people simply because it makes them feel good.

In order to relate to the feelings of others, children also need to be comfortable with their own emotions. Whether they express hostility, anger, fear, sadness, joy, silliness, or pity, children's integrity can be honored by parents who show respect for their children's emotions. Unfortunately, some parents are often uncomfortable with their children's emotions for many reasons. They may deny or suppress their own strong feelings, or a child's emotions may remind them of things they don't like about themselves. Parents may be frustrated by feeling that they aren't getting through to a child, they may experience strong emotions of their own in response to a child's pain, or they may feel guilty for causing a child's emotional pain. Or perhaps they are just too tired to deal with emotional upsets.

Some typical responses from parents who are inadvertently teaching their kids to deny their own emotions may include:

> "Oh Gerald, how can you say you hate your little brother? You know you don't really mean that." (When, at that moment, he really *is* furious.)
>
> "Don't worry about missing your old friends. When we move into our new neighborhood, you'll make a lot of new ones." (When he's feeling too vulnerable to venture out.)
>
> "Don't be afraid of the dog, Elizabeth. He won't hurt you. You're just being a 'fraidy cat.'" (When, in fact, she's terrified.)

In each case a parent is dismissing the legitimacy of the child's concerns, saying in essence that their fears are trivial and inappropriate. Here are some more effective responses that acknowledge the validity of a child's feelings, without judgment or denial. *Only after expressing empathy* does each parent offer reassurance or propose a constructive way to deal with a problem:

> "Sometimes you feel angry toward your brother, Gerald. I understand that. But you cannot express your anger

by hitting him. Why don't you pound your fist into this pillow to show me just how angry you feel?''

"I know you are sad about leaving your friends behind. I'm going to miss my friends, too. It won't be easy for us, but we'll be able to talk to them on the telephone, and perhaps we'll come back to visit. And I hope we will be able to meet nice people in our new neighborhood. I will try to help make it easier for you by setting up something to meet our new neighbors.''

"I know that you sometimes are frightened by dogs, Elizabeth. And that's a big one over there. But that dog belongs to Melinda's family and I know he is very gentle. I'll go over first and show you that he's friendly. Then maybe you'll come over with me.''

## The Value of Household Chores

Some parents are reluctant to assign their children tasks to complete at home, reasoning, "School should be the only job they have," "I had to do too much when I was their age and I want my kids to be kids," "I have to do it all over again anyway because they don't do things right," or even "We can afford to hire help, so why should the kids have to lend a hand?" Other parents, on the other hand, ask their children to take on too much responsibility too soon, expecting young kids to care for even younger siblings on a regular basis.

Finding a balance between these two extremes is necessary to instill a healthy sense of responsibility. Most experts agree that parents who do not assign any chores to their children are depriving them of a valuable lesson in the importance of interdependency. While children resent busy work, they like to know that they are needed and appreciated. With two working parents so commonplace these days, children can certainly be a vital part of the family team in helping to keep things running smoothly. Assigning age-appropriate chores sends a message that says: "In this household, we all help each other. Our cooperative efforts allow each one of us to thrive. And every contribution is valuable."

Shouldering the responsibility of chores also teaches a child how a household is run. This provides educational opportunities, too. For example, asking a four-year-old to match socks according to color while you fold the laundry is a great way to reinforce nursery school lessons. Coming home from the grocery store with a dozen paper sacks filled with food gives everyone a chance to help unload the car. Even though six-year-old Julia can only manage one small bag at a time, she shares an essential family duty and, at the same time, learns that food doesn't magically appear on refrigerator shelves or on the table.

Young children are most enthusiastic about helping with household chores when it gives them some extra time with their parents. One mother admits that her daughters, ages 2½ and four, are often more of a hindrance than a help, but her goal is to set a pattern for the future: "I let them 'help Mommy' make the beds, bake cookies, set the table, and dry the dishes. I don't want to discourage them even at this tender age. Right now it seems like fun to them, and if we set the pattern at this age, maybe it won't seem like such a burden to them when they are older."

The best way to introduce children to new assignments is to work closely with them. For example, when Robyn was four, her parents felt she was old enough to put away her own toys and decided to introduce the concept in three stages. First, her father put away the toys in Robyn's presence, explaining in the process that toys needed to be returned to the shelf so they would not get lost or start to clutter the house. Then, father and daughter began spending 10 minutes together every evening cleaning up her room. Finally, Robyn was told that she was ready to put her own toys away every night. That was a proud moment for Robyn, who saw it as an important step toward independence. Now, her parents say, whenever a neighbor's child comes over to play, Robyn explains the rules about putting away toys.

Regardless of the results, parents should try to remember always to praise a child's sincere efforts. Chances are that the first time a child volunteers to set the table, she'll forget at least some of the flatware and may not arrange the plates the way a parent wants them. Thank her anyway. (''Good job, Tanya. You stepped right in to help out when you saw how busy I was with dinner. I appreciate that.'') The parent can then explain how she likes to see the table set: ''Let's count the forks and make sure everyone has one. It looks as if we'd better bring two more forks to the table.'' These positive remarks confirm Tanya's accomplishment and establish a friendly tone that makes her receptive to gentle corrections. The next time, Tanya is more likely to count the forks herself and set the table just right.

Here are some other suggestions for getting children to help with household chores, while providing a learning opportunity at the same time:

- **Assign chores at an early age.** As children get older, the ball game down the street, a favorite television show, or just hanging out with friends will all seem more tempting than contributing around the house. It becomes much harder to establish good work habits in preteens than in preschoolers.
- **When a child first takes on a new chore, don't worry about efficiency.** Genuine effort is more important. Be quick to praise it.

- **To avoid frustrating or discouraging a child, be certain that assigned chores are appropriate to her age and capabilities.** It is often helpful to provide child-size tools. A small broom or rake, a lightweight watering can, or a stool she can stand on while helping to wash the car each allow her to participate more fully.

- **Establish the importance of a child's contribution to the team effort of running a household.** A child needs to know why her work is so important ("Thanks, Kari, for helping me chop the vegetables. Your work helped me serve dinner on time"). Parents might also let a child know that if work gets done quickly, there will be extra time for fun family activities.

- **Establish a checklist.** Letting children cross off each chore or placing a gold star next to a job description when it is completed gives children a tangible sense of accomplishment. Instead of nagging about uncompleted chores, parents can ask, "Have you been able to check off all your jobs for today?"

- **If parents do need to remind children about chores or want to assign new responsibilities, time requests carefully.** Parents will find it easier to get cooperation when children are not hungry, tired, or busy with some other activity. If parents interrupt when children are concentrating on something else, this might fuel resentment rather than foster cooperation.

- **Parents may also encourage more cooperation by allowing some flexibility in chores when possible.** For those chores that do not need to be done at a specific time, let children choose their own time to do the work. If a child works out her own way to do a chore, let her continue to do so as long as her way gets the job done. If children want to trade or rotate chores, allow them to do so, again, so long as the job gets done.

After taking a look at what roles they have filled and would like to fill with their children, some parents may lose heart and think that they have already let too many opportunities go by for teaching responsibility and that it's too late to start. However, it's never too late to start making appropriate changes. With older children, parents may need a great deal more patience and may have to provide more explanations as to why things have to change. Perhaps, however, by admitting to themselves and to their children that everyone lets things slide, and that becoming responsible is not easy for children or adults but that it does have its rewards, even the most chaotic family has a chance to achieve an atmosphere of responsibility.

• • • • • • • • • • • • • • • • • • • • • • • • • • • • • • • •

## Parents ask:

*I was brought up to be terribly responsible, and I feel that I never had the kind of carefree childhood that a kid deserves. My own mother is horrified that I let my daughter watch television before doing her homework and that I really don't ask too much in terms of chores. But my daughter is a much happier child than I ever was. I've come to the conclusion that a child's only responsibility is to be a child. Am I wrong? Is my mother right?*

The truth is, they're both right. This mother is not wrong to want to try to give her child what she considers a happier childhood than she had. However, when a parent creates parenting guidelines for herself that are the exact opposite of what her parents did (as most of us do in some way or another because almost all of us do at least a few things differently from our parents), she ends up creating a policy that may be too rigid. In this case, the parent loses her ability to respond flexibly. She also runs the risk of being completely overpowered by her child. To create a policy of no chores prevents a child from learning responsibility or having the privilege of pulling her weight around the house. Part of being a kid is learning how to do chores. If nothing is demanded of a child at home, she may find herself unable to take part in activities in other areas of life where she is required to do her fair share. By striking a balance between her own childhood difficulties and her child's needs, this mother can help her child grow.

# PART II

......

# Day by Day with Your Responsible Child

"EDDIE AND I ARE GOING TO BE BEST FRIENDS AS SOON AS WE GET THE KINKS IRONED OUT."

# CHAPTER THREE

•••••

# First, There's the Family

An answer to a child's question of "Who am I?" may be as simple as saying, "You're a member of our family." To become healthy and responsible adults, children need to be full participants in family life, including all the interactions of day-to-day communication, competition, and cooperation every family experiences. Well-known humorist Erma Bombeck described her brood in *Family: The Ties That Bind . . . and Gag!* as "a strange little band of characters trudging through life sharing disease and toothpaste, coveting one another's desserts, hiding shampoo, borrowing money, locking each other out of our rooms, inflicting pain and kissing to heal it in the same instant, loving, laughing, defending, and trying to figure out the common thread that bound us all together."

Whatever group environment children find themselves in later in life, the skills they need to succeed at life begin in the family. It is at home that children find their first opportunities to learn to give and receive love, abilities that will enhance *all* future relationships.

Home life also offers the best chance to learn good communication skills. Long before a child has uttered his first word, he's learned about listening. Parents who really listen, in turn, help a child gain the ability to listen without judging. A child who knows that his opinions are heard and respected is likely to have a secure sense of personal worth. Asking questions, discussing issues large and small, and making one's needs known are all part of the communication process. The tools for successful negotiation also begin at home. The way parents settle arguments and the way they teach their children to negotiate for what they want lay the groundwork for a lifetime of fruitful relationships. Conflicts are most effectively resolved when people make an effort to understand opposing points of view and are willing to compromise.

Learning how to be a team player begins not on a sports field but in a home where each member has learned to carry his share of responsibility, including the responsibility of being a sibling. Siblings need not be each other's closest friends, but they need to be taught to value the uniqueness of their relationship and take strength from it, while learning to care for each other.

Finally, the adult skill of being able to handle money wisely begins in the grade-school years. Whether a child receives a weekly allowance or earns his own money through such activities as baby-sitting, mowing lawns, or working in the community, he can begin early to appreciate the value of a dollar, the benefits of saving, and the art of living within a budget.

Armed with this set of skills, children can develop into adults who are capable of negotiating the adult world of work and who are able to sustain mature relationships. In *A Guide to a Happier Family*, Andrew Schwebel, Ph.D., and others describe the ideals of grown-ups: ''You are trusting of those you love when you can bare your soul without fear of embarrassment or humiliation. You are capable of intimacy when, knowing you love someone, you are able to express it; when troubled by something your mate has said or done, you can talk openly about it; or when as an adult you are still treated as a child by your parents, you are able to set them straight with loving firmness rather than hostility.'' We do not achieve all of these ideals all of the time, but keeping them in mind can help us work toward them.

## Family Style

As they live from day to day, families usually do not consciously think they represent any particular style. All most parents want is to be able to get through the day with a minimum amount of conflict and a maximum amount of peace and joy. However, this desire is communicated to children in many different ways, depending on how the family operates. The style of operation is influenced by the family's cultural, economic, and ethnic background. In American society a great range of styles can be seen, from permissive to restrictive, from close-knit to cold and distant. While few disagree that a close-knit style is preferable to one that is cold, debate continues about which discipline style—authoritarian or permissive—is best for kids.

The best style, not surprisingly, has been found to be one that falls between these two extremes. Midrange, *authoritative* (not authoritarian) families, often dubbed *democratic*, consistently produce the most socially responsible children. In democratic families, parents practice control while encouraging open communication.

The term *democratic*, as applied to families, does not mean a society in which every member has an equal vote. It does mean that every member has input into rules and decision making. The amount and type of input encouraged from children varies with the kids' ages and abilities, but even young children in democratic families are afforded some explanation of rules and are allowed to make some decisions of their own. As described by authors Dr. Michael Schulman and Eva Mekler in *Bringing*

*Up a Moral Child:* "In democratic families, the child followed the rules because he believed his parents' reasons made sense. When a child felt his parents' explanations weren't sound, he wasn't expected to simply accept them; they were open to discussion. Moreover, children who were raised democratically and given reasons for rules turned out to be the most self-confident and independent adolescents."

The idea of running a family on the basis of fair discussion, negotiation, and compromise sounds wonderful to most people. However, what looks good in theory often does not prove so in reality when a parent is confronted with a child's argument that a given rule is "unfair." Parents can become angry and exhausted by unsuccessful and time-consuming attempts to negotiate. Some parents also may say that the democratic model is fine for families with young children, but nearly impossible to introduce into a family with older children where attitudes and habits already seem so firmly in place. However, for a family set in uncomfortable ways, most members will agree that there could be improvements. It's never too late to begin exploring ways to communicate more effectively and operate in a more equitable manner.

## Opening the Lines of Communication

A child who learns to express his feelings and ask for what he wants—without bullying, whining, manipulating, or becoming hostile—masters an art with a lifetime of usefulness. Good communication also extends to the ability to keep an open mind while listening to and respecting the expressions of others and then being able to respond in a clear, empathic manner.

Good communication helps keep a family running smoothly and prevents misunderstandings from escalating into conflict or from being buried unresolved. But communication won't happen unless both parents and children feel they are allowed to express themselves and know that their ideas will be heard and considered. Communication failure is often evidenced in complaints from parents that their children, especially teenagers, will not listen to anything they say. And children complain that their parents don't care what they say or yell at them if they bring up a sensitive issue. When questioned by outside researchers, many parents and children express frustration at their inability to communicate, wishing that it were easier to have a meaningful exchange of ideas, feelings, and concerns.

In *Voices of Hope,* part of a book trilogy called *Teenagers Themselves,* some teenagers had this to say about communication with their parents:

> "I think it would be neat if your mother would tell you something about herself and ask you to tell her something. You could bring out your inner selves."

> "Sharing your lives is the basis for preventing the communication gap. If I went home and my parents weren't interested in what I did, we would have a bigger communication gap."

> "Anytime I go to my dad, he says, 'I don't really have time to listen to this.' . . . My mom said, 'He cares, but he just can't show it. That's the way he was brought up.' I think, 'Gosh, sometimes he could show it instead of ignoring me.' "

> "You need an open mind. One of the coolest people I know is my adopted grandmother. She's 80 or so, and she's able to talk about anything: sex, drugs, or whatever. She hasn't gone through it, but she's open to talk, which is something that my parents still aren't able to do."

The comments from parents reflect some of the same barriers:

> "My wife tells me that my son wants so much for me to be proud of him. But he never shares his activities with me. Usually he just answers 'Nothing' when I ask him what he's been doing. Or he says I'm trying to pry into his personal life."
>
> "I often ask my daughter 'What's wrong?' if I think she's upset about something. Her usual reply is, 'Oh, Mom, you wouldn't understand.' I know teenagers face a lot of things today I never had to deal with, but I wish she'd remember that I *was* her age at one time. I might actually be able to help her with something."

Clearly, the desire for communication is present on both sides. What the comments suggest is that both parents and children have a lot to learn about opening and keeping open the channels of communication between them.

To set the stage for communication, parents need to begin early to encourage children to share confidences. If a pattern of communication is established early, when children's concerns are less earth-shattering, it will be easier to maintain as they grow older and issues assume greater significance. For example, a parent might take the time to ask a three- or four-year-old about what he liked best about a visit with friends, why he likes a particular toy, what he thought when he laughed at a clown, what made him angry with the baby or sad about a friend, or why he doesn't like to go to bed.

Time for family dialogues and for private one-to-one parent-child conversations also helps. These encounters don't have to be formal "Let's sit down and talk" times. They often are most successful when they happen within a natural context. For example, a parent might take one child to get a sandwich at a local hamburger place or ask him to help clean the garage or do the dishes. When the purpose of the get-together is not centered on the need to talk, conversation usually will flow more naturally. Rather than start in with a specific topic, parents may try asking a child what he wants to talk about. One mother said that she and her eight-year-old son talked about a lot of things when he went with her to the store: "One day we passed a music store and he mentioned that it bothered him that he and his best friend didn't like the same kind of music. We turned it into a great conversation about how people with different likes and dislikes could still be friends and what kind of music I liked when I was a kid."

A natural setting for family dialogues is the dinner table. If conversation doesn't flow freely, parents might want to start with a topic or have each family member ask another person a question. Once everyone is comfortable expressing himself, parents should encourage discussions of problems family members are having, such as a strict teacher, an angry girlfriend or co-worker, an upcoming test, or a playmate who doesn't share. Of course, not every dinnertime will turn out to be filled with friendly talk and sharing. In normal families, children often interrupt, tease each other, criticize the food, and don't listen. Parents need to keep trying. Communication will happen, often unexpectedly, and family members will feel closer as a result.

Some families find that having a regular meeting helps to air problems, discuss chores, and make plans for family activities. These meetings might be scheduled or occur whenever an issue needs to be handled. Some parents may want to talk with individual children before the meeting to determine what the feelings are surrounding a particular issue. The meeting itself is likely to go more smoothly if parents set rules to guide the discussion, such as no interruptions or name-calling, and if they clearly state the topic.

Everyone needs to be allowed to express an opinion and suggest solutions or ideas.

Talking frankly about emotions and anxieties is a source of strength, not an admission of weakness. In families where "keeping a stiff upper lip" is perceived as a virtue, children may repress strong feelings or become reticent about speaking openly. As a result, they may find it difficult to acknowledge emotions in themselves or others or to ask for help when they need it. Misunderstandings may also remain unresolved. For example, nine-year-old Jennifer was told by her parents to be a big girl and not be so upset when her parakeet flew away. As a result, she had no outlet or guidance for her grief. In contrast, when 11-year-old Greg confessed that he was nervous about his first camp-out with his scout troop, *his* father didn't tell him he was being silly or that he needed to be brave. Instead he told Greg it was normal to feel anxious about any anticipated new experience. They sat down and talked about what expectations Greg had about camping that scared him. "I found out that he had read a magazine article about a camper being attacked by a wild animal," the father said. "We talked about the wildlife that lived in the area where he would be camping and the fact that most animals want to stay as far away from humans as they can."

Listening closely to a child's description of an event and encouraging him to express his reactions encourages communication. By doing so, the child will learn to trust his perceptions and how his feelings relate to what happened. For example, when Melanie came home with a story about how all the 10-year-old boys ran into the clubhouse and locked her out, her mother listened and acknowledged Melanie's feelings:

MOM: That must have made you feel angry.
MELANIE: It sure did.

MOM: Maybe you're afraid it will happen again.

MELANIE: No way. I've got plenty of my own friends. I don't need to be with anyone who is so mean.

By talking about her feelings, Melanie was better able to resolve them herself.

It is easy and normal to take people for granted, but parents need to try to remember to make every member of the family feel that his opinions, ideas, and interests are worthwhile. If a child feels valued, he will be more willing to share himself in the form of communication. For example, 15-year-old Carla has won an award at school, while 5-year-old Henry has finally learned to set the dinner table just right. Each accomplishment should be acknowledged as important. A parent might consider praising each accomplishment before the whole family, as well as giving an encouraging hug in private.

Parents who find it difficult to communicate with a quiet or withdrawn child may need to face a problem head-on by approaching the child directly. When 14-year-old Tom seemed to be having trouble with his grades, his mother tried everything she could think of to get him to talk about it. Finally she directly told him that as a parent she was concerned about his schoolwork, and she asked him why he wouldn't talk to her. He reluctantly told her he was afraid she would tell him that his difficulties were all his fault. Once she understood why he was uncommunicative, Tom's mother was able to help him think of different ways to approach his school problem.

## Nonverbal Communication

Nonverbal reassurance and physical contact also are vital to a healthy childhood. Nonverbal communication can be as simple as an encouraging smile and as reassuring as a firm hug.

The importance of touch in infancy has been well established, and its soothing impact is evident. Less well known is the continuing need for bonding throughout childhood and indeed during the entire course of a person's life. The secure attachment between parent and child, which has so much to do with a child's later ability to develop close social ties, must not be neglected as the child moves beyond infancy. Receiving a hug is just as necessary for an adolescent to feel valued and secure as it is for a toddler.

Some parents feel uncomfortable with physical contact when their children approach adolescence and sexual maturity. They may pull away unconsciously, especially from an opposite-sex child. Even if they do so consciously, parents may be unable to explain their actions. As a result, children may be confused or worried that they have done something to upset the parent. Conversely, children may pull away as they mature, leaving parents feeling hurt and rejected.

By pulling away physically from their growing children, parents may miss opportunities to help children develop healthy attitudes about the continuing need for normal human affection. To counteract this tendency, parents first can realize that withdrawal from physical contact on the part of both parents and adolescents is normal. Parents may be uncomfortable with any reminders that their children are sexual beings, and children will see any physical contact with their parents as "not cool," especially around peers or siblings. Parents can keep in touch by continuing to offer physical contact, but only when a child wants it. They also may need to redefine physical contact. Whereas with young children it may have meant frequent and spontaneous displays of affection, with older children it may be just sitting quietly near each other, giving a hug, or voicing affection. Adolescents may still give affection spontaneously, but parents will have to let them decide when. Discretion and timing are important with young people, who often are ruled by roller coaster moods.

## The Art of Negotiation

Harmonious negotiation takes place in an atmosphere of mutual respect, in which all parties feel they can come away with something rather than feel they're in a win-lose situation. While confrontation may work well in a courtroom, it only fuels resentment and limits communication within a family.

Promoting compromise and candor in a spirit of fairness is the most effective way to reconcile differences. This means understanding that people have conflicting needs and differing perspectives. To reach a common ground, all parties first must state their needs and wishes, listen to the needs and wishes of others, then finally work together to find an acceptable solution. Most parents know that such a process is rarely without pitfalls, especially when children are likely to think of their own wishes as primary and those of parents and siblings as secondary.

In family negotiations, parents need to remind themselves that an effort to be fair is important—especially since most adolescents will consider unfair any rule they don't like. However, parents also need to remind themselves that they *are* the ones in charge. They have the right to say no, and they should not feel compelled to negotiate everything. As Dr. Thomas Lickona writes in *Raising Good Children*, "Kids will generally accept your assertions of authority as being fair as long as you give a reason when one is needed, grant them a fair hearing when they want one, and try to work out fair solutions when real conflicts arise." However, he cautions parents to "be clear when you need simple obedience or cooperation."

Dr. Lickona also offers a three-part method for negotiating with children. First he suggests "achieving mutual understanding" by stating the purpose of the negotiation, stating both points of view, describing the problem, and paraphrasing each other's feelings. Secondly he suggests "solving the problem" by making a list of possible solutions, writing down what both parties think is fair, then following up to see if the agreement is working. Finally he suggests "following through" to talk about how effective the plan has been.

Here is an example of how this process might work:

In the Wallach family, nine-year-old Jesse washes the dishes after dinner every evening and 12-year-old Meghan is responsible for checking the refrigerator for staples and walking to the store to buy them whenever necessary. When there is no milk in the refrigerator for the second day in a row, Mrs. Wallach calls a family conference:

MOM: What's happening, Meghan? It's frustrating to come home and have no milk in the refrigerator for dinner.

MEGHAN: Well, when I have basketball practice after school, our coach gives some of us a ride home, and we don't pass the store.

MOM: I can understand that you can't get to the store before dinner on the days when you have basketball practice. But this is a job you agreed to do. Do you understand how I feel?

MEGHAN: You're annoyed. But it's not fair. Why can't Jesse go to the store sometimes?

JESSE: No! I'm not going to the store in the afternoon *and* washing the dishes every night.

MOM: Let's each write down some of our ideas for solving this problem so we can have milk in the house, clean dishes, and Meghan can still go to basketball practice. Then we'll talk about it.

Mom didn't introduce the problem in an angry way. Instead, she expressed concern and asked for an explanation. She also accepted Meghan's explanation, but reminded her of her commitment and asked her to consider other family members' feelings. The three of them finally settle on Meghan and Jesse switching chores on the days Meghan has basketball practice. They then agree to talk about it in one week and then again in two weeks to see if the new arrangement is working. If not, they will have to talk about other ways to solve the problem.

Parents could resort to a modified plan with younger children, also adapted from Dr. Lickona, that uses questions to help them work through the problem. For example, a parent might ask a child who is being disruptive at the table, "What are you doing?" The child might reply, "Kicking the table." The parent might then ask, "What should you be doing?" or "What's the rule about how to sit at the table?" Whether or not the child immediately responds with proper behavior, he at least is made to think about his actions and possibly the consequences.

## A Member of the Team

"We must all hang together or we will assuredly each hang alone," Benjamin Franklin declared at the signing of the Declaration of Independence. That assertion remains true today. The concept that a family is a team in which everyone contributes something for the greater good of all is one that parents will find effective in trying to foster day-to-day cooperation and caring in their children. By the age of five, most children can begin to understand the idea of teamwork and will enjoy feeling a part of a larger group effort.

Before introducing the team concept, however, parents need to consider some fundamental differences between an actual team and a real family. On a team all members have one stated need and goal: to win. In a family the major goal is striving to be a smoothly functioning group that helps all members feel fulfilled. But in a family, as opposed to a team, the members also are individuals with separate lives who are interested in their *own* success and development. Parents will find that their family team won't always pull together, especially when individuals' needs conflict. However, the idea of pulling together can be used to lessen some conflicts and to encourage children to consider other family members' feelings and desires.

In a family team, members fully participate by doing all they can to stay healthy and safe, taking care of their own possessions, and pitching in to keep the household running effectively. Contributing to the running of the household takes into account the fact that everyone has to share the household space and that doing one's part keeps this space more pleasant for all. For example, by cleaning up after themselves in the kitchen, helping to keep the living room picked up, and keeping their own rooms relatively neat (or at least remembering to close the door on chaos), children show that they value and respect their home and are considerate of other family members' desire to live in a nice environment.

Team players are mature enough to heed established household rules, assertive enough to negotiate change when appropriate, and secure enough to be accountable to their teammates. The mother of an eight-year-old boy explains it this way: "If my son wants to go bike riding with his friends, he is told when he is expected back. We let him know that we believe he is responsible enough to follow our guidelines. Should he violate our trust, then the privilege of bike riding will have to be revoked. We try to communicate the message that members of a family who love each other will not deliberately cause one another unnecessary worry."

A spirit of team effort can be fostered in many ways and tailored to the age and abilities of children. Whenever possible, children should be encouraged to support each other at personal events, such as going to a brother's baseball game or a school play in which a sister has a part. Young children ordinarily take part in family events, but teenagers also should be encouraged strongly to attend a certain number of family gatherings. These gatherings may include frequent dinners together; a weekend activity, such as church attendance; an occasional family picnic; or a once-a-month movie. Parents may find resistance on the part of teenagers who are more interested in spending time with their friends, and parents should be willing to compromise on some activities. They should also consider which activities they feel need whole family participation and stress to their teenagers how important these get-togethers are in keeping the sense of family strong. Though older kids may balk, they also realize that parents' insistence on their presence says, in effect, "You're fun to have around."

Another way to nurture teamwork is to make sure children realize the benefits of working together. As one mother of two says, "Our children have learned that with cooperation chores get done faster, leaving more time for play and other fun things. One day they wanted to go on a picnic, but I said I had too much work to do around the house. They decided that going on a picnic was worth helping me clean, and so they pitched in. Before I knew it, we were out the door and on our way."

During certain phases of their lives, many children are likely to behave as if they want to quit the family team. The summer when a teenager asks to skip the family vacation to stay home and work, for example, is a jolting reminder of his growing autonomy. Erma Bombeck puts a light-hearted perspective on teenagers in "*Just Wait Till You Have Children of Your Own!*": "Our teen-agers withdrew to their bedrooms on their thirteenth birthday and didn't show themselves to us again until it was time to get married. If we spoke to them in public, they threatened to self-destruct within three minutes.''

Like any organic unit, the family must be flexible enough to accommodate the changing needs of its members. A child's need to assume more responsibility may entail allowing him to go his own way if parents feel he is old enough and they can trust him. By not being made to feel guilty for growing up, a child may eventually return to the family as an eager participant—at least once in a while. Learning to let go a little does not mean losing touch with a newly independent child, however. Parents still need to communicate to find out whether or not the child is meeting his responsibilities, how he is doing emotionally, and whether or not he needs any help. They also may still insist on his frequent presence at dinnertime, for example, and he should still be invited to all family gatherings.

## The Question of Privacy

The members of every family, if they live in the same household, share their lives to a certain extent in a limited space. Children's desire for independence can turn the home into a battleground. Many young people, for example, become resentful of parental questioning and what they perceive to be prying into their personal lives. Parents, too, often feel bombarded by their children's constant demands—ones that leave parents little or no private time.

Privacy is a delicate issue. When children are very young, parents think longingly of having even a few minutes to themselves. As children leave babyhood, they begin to crave privacy of their own. Respecting this mutual need for privacy is another part of the team effort in running a family. A young child needs to be taught that although Mom and Dad are never very far away, they sometimes need a few moments by themselves. Parents also can respect their child's right to privacy as a way of communicating their trust in him. Allowing him to keep some of the details of his life private and providing him space that is safely off-limits to the prying eyes of outsiders help him assert his independence and advance the necessary process of separation from his parents.

Siblings who have to share a room can be encouraged to work out between themselves a system that allows each of them some privacy. This may include an arrangement in which each sibling is allowed a certain amount of time alone in the room or a searching out of other places in the house where time alone might be spent. In the case of a sibling agreement, parents should check that the agreed-upon solution is as fair as possible to both parties. Parents also may have to deal with arguments over how the room should look. One child may be neat, while the other may be sloppy. There may be a problem with siblings getting into each other's things. Easy and permanent solutions to a peaceful sharing of space are hard to find. Many ideas may have to be tried before a workable one is found, but parents should always insist that their children respect the rights of others to keep a room as they see fit and to have private places and property within the room.

Parents also may wonder just how much they should tell children about any financial or marital problems they or a relative may be having or how much of their personal feelings they should share with their children. Most children who are school-age and older want to know about matters that concern the whole family, and most such children are capable of understanding the need for keeping family matters private outside the home. If a parent comes home consistently cranky, he might explain, ''I'm having a problem with one of my co-workers.'' While demonstrating that everyone, even parents, has problems, this kind of sharing also reassures children that they themselves are not the source of such problems.

Some privacy guidelines are relatively easy to establish. Everyone should knock before entering a family member's room. Neither parents nor siblings have the right to read each other's mail, use or invade personal possessions, or read someone's diary. Such violations, writes Dr. Haim G. Ginott in *Between Parent and Teenager*, ''may cause permanent resentment. Teenagers feel cheated and enraged. In their eyes, invasion of privacy is a dishonorable offense.'' And rightly so in *most* situations.

Trickier to deal with is the extent to which parents should allow a school-age or teenage child to remain uncommunicative. Is a child obliged to tell his parents where he has been or who is telephoning him? How much should parents probe into his daily (and later, his evening) activities? What are parents entitled to know about his dates? Answers can be formulated only individually within each family, in consultation with all involved parties. A parent's prime objective is to balance the child's right to privacy with the obligation to protect his safety.

On some occasions it is unquestionably a parental duty to pry. When parents pick up signals that their child is in trouble of some sort, allowing him to remain uncommunicative is no longer an act of respect but one of irresponsibility. Ideally a child who is comfortable with the level of privacy he is generally awarded will understand and perhaps even welcome his parents' probing into a specific issue of concern. Whether his response is hostile or not, any indication that he is having serious academic or disciplinary problems at school, that he is abusing drugs or alcohol, or that he is engaging in risky sexual activities signals the moment that safety concerns must take precedence over the child's right to privacy.

## Cultivating the Sibling Bond

The bonds between siblings are marked by a sometimes odd, sometimes maddening, often-touching blend of loyalty, bossiness, protectiveness, and cruelty. The relationship changes over the years, and often from day to day and even hour by hour. Bickering is inevitable, and there are generally phases of rivalry and deep antagonism as well. Nonetheless, siblings who learn to trust each other, to respect each other's rights within the family unit, and to assume responsibility for each other's well-being cement a bond that lasts a lifetime. At its best, the sibling relationship is one of the most rewarding and intimate interpersonal connections of adulthood.

Reflecting on the ever-changing dynamics between her five- and three-year-old sons, one mother notes: "They play together in the backyard, and Marty will let me know if Joey begins to wander off toward the road. When friends come over, however, the mood sometimes shifts. On a good day, Marty might say, 'Don't hit Joey; he's littler than us and we should be nice to him.' On other days, and for no apparent reason, I've also heard him declare with glee, 'Let's throw leaves on Joey's head.'"

While all parents prefer their children to be kind to each other—and taunting sibling cruelty can sometimes become a real problem—there's nothing unusual about the shifting moods of Marty and Joey's relationship. As their mother observed philosophically, "They don't take care of each other every minute of the day, but if anything really happened to the other one, I know they'd act responsibly."

What can parents do to cultivate sibling loyalty rather than rivalry? How can they encourage their children to feel an appropriate level of responsibility for the well-being of their siblings? Some suggestions:

- **Be prepared for the tempestuous changes that the birth of a sibling can bring to a family.** No matter how well parents try to prepare an older child, there is likely to be a rocky period of adjustment before the older child regains his equilibrium and feels secure again. This jealousy may be toned down somewhat by parents' efforts to pay extra attention to the older child and to involve him as much as possible in the care of the new baby by giving him specific jobs to do. Parents might also talk to the child in order to help him name the jealous or angry feelings he may be having.

- **Accept the inevitability of sibling spats and don't try to force children to like each other.** Siblings commonly go through phases during which they are relatively close and other times when they are somewhat more distant. Within reason, name-calling, taunts such as "Go away, this is only for big kids," and even physical fights are a normal part of growing up and usually are not a cause for alarm. However, more personal and insulting put-downs, which are also common, should not be accepted; nor should real violence be tolerated. Dr. Thomas Lickona suggests that parents make clear to their children that someone who behaves intolerably toward another human being reveals his *own* insecurities, that other people are unlikely to forget certain insults and will continue to think badly of the one who has hurt them, and that put-downs can weaken another person's self-esteem.

- **Within limits, encourage siblings to do things for each other.** Now and then an older sibling can take care of a younger one so long as the older child is still allowed time with peers of his own age group and is not asked to take on too much responsibility. Asking children to help out with one another can cement the trust, support, and love that is possible among brothers and sisters. For instance, as a toddler, Mark brought diapers when sister Sarah had to be changed and liked to sing to her as she fell asleep. A pattern of protectiveness was established early in their lives, and even as adults, Mark and Sarah continue the habit of looking out for each other. However, most siblings are not consistently protective and parents should accept that there will be times when their children do not take care of each other.

- **Treat each child as an individual with separate interests and talents.** Praise each child's accomplishments and make it clear that every member of the family has opportunities to be the star. However, do not relegate children to certain roles by labeling them. According to Adele Faber and Elaine Mazlish, authors of *Siblings Without Rivalry*, by always calling one child ''responsible,'' for example, and another child ''forgetful'' or ''charmer'' or ''athlete,'' parents may unwittingly set expectations that children feel compelled to try to live up to. As a result, some children may feel they can't or won't be responsible because another sibling is already so good at it and they don't want their efforts to be compared with the champ's. The responsible children, in turn, may feel they always have to be responsible and may feel guilty and anxious when they don't measure up. Siblings can carry these labels even into adult life.

## Tattling

''I'm telling on you.'' What parent hasn't heard one child say that to another? Sooner or later, brothers and sisters begin tattling on each other. There's a fine line between teaching children to report incidents that are dangerous or unethical—that's responsible behavior—and encouraging them to tattle. "Sometimes they tell me things they are right to tell, like when Tony was playing with matches near a pile of leaves," points out one father. Parents also have to contend sometimes with sibling loyalty, in which one child agonizes over whether to tell a parent that a sibling is in trouble, wishing to protect the sibling from parental anger.

On the other hand, tattling is often used as a tactic for one child to gain the upper hand over the other. It's important not to get too caught up in the tattletale game or to let children use their arguments as a way of getting parental attention. When they come to a parent with a trivial dispute over toys and the parent can readily establish that no one is either physically or emotionally getting hurt, it is usually best to urge them to work it out for themselves. Trying to find out "who did it" or playing judge is often an impossible task. Here's some familiar-sounding bickering:

"Alex took my baseball glove."
"I did it because he hit me."
"Well, I hit him because he wouldn't move off the baseball field when we were right in the middle of the game."
(*Sighs their father.*) "There's no way I can possibly figure out who really started the fight or who is at fault, so I'll usually say, 'You guys are not cooperating with each other. I think you should both go to your room for 10 minutes and think about it.' "

Declares another father of two: "There is no profit in taking sides. You have no way of knowing what really happened. If they are fighting over a toy and each accuses the other of grabbing it, I'll say 'Let's put the toy away for now. Toys are for playing and having fun with, and that's obviously not what's happening right now, so you two had better find something else to do.' ''

Once children discover that tattling won't win them any extra points with Mom and Dad, they find it easier to stop. That puts the responsibility for getting along back where it belongs: squarely on children's shoulders.

## Arguments

Sometimes children argue incessantly over possessions or use of the television, or they may tease each other to the point of tears and/or blows. The aggressor may not want parental intervention—which might get him in trouble and prevent him from getting his way—and the victim might be too intimidated to say anything. If serious arguing erupts, parents need to gauge how serious the argument is and step in if necessary.

For their parent workshops, Adele Faber and Elaine Mazlish have developed steps that parents might use once they determine that an argument between two children is more than normal bickering. They recommend that ''if the situation is heating up, adult intervention might be helpful.'' To do so, parents need to ''acknowledge children's anger, reflect each child's point of view, describe the problem with respect, express confidence in the children's ability to find their own solution, then leave the room.'' If the argument escalates into a possibly dangerous situation, they recommend that parents need to find out if it is a play fight or a real fight. Parents should insist that ''play fighting is allowed by mutual consent only.'' If intervention is necessary, they suggest that parents describe what they see, then separate the children and have them spend time away from each other in order to cool off. Parents can then help children think of other ways for expressing their anger than by hitting each other. This might include writing down or practicing saying what they feel ("I'm angry that you borrowed my shirt without asking me first") or finding some other activity as an outlet for high emotions, such as taking a walk. Siblings also need to be encouraged to consider each other's feelings, to apologize when appropriate, and to remember that life isn't always fair.

## Finances Within the Family

Throughout their dealings with each other and with parents, children learn how to make reasoned judgments and decisions, how to take care of themselves, and how to care about others. The family also is the basis for another vital survival skill: having a healthy, responsible attitude toward money.

In our materialistic society, one of the toughest challenges parents face is how to instill appropriate respect for the value of a dollar. Children are barraged by advertising— for the latest toy, the sweetest breakfast cereal, the hottest new outfit. They go to school with other children who show off recently purchased acquisitions, wander wistfully through clothing stores, and peer wide-eyed at store shelves piled high with new games. The quest for money of their own intensifies during the teen years, when they discover makeup, music, fast food, leather jackets, and other paraphernalia they deem indispensable.

In the face of all of these consumer temptations and the prevalent attitude about the power and glamour of money, how can parents teach their children to be responsible with money? How can children be taught that money can't buy happiness or friends or love, that there are more important values than money, and that there is a limit to family finances?

Parents might want to begin by remembering that the ultimate deprivation is no deprivation at all: children don't prosper by getting everything they want as soon as they ask for it. Influenced by the desire to provide a good life for children, or simply by a child's sheer persistence, many parents find it difficult to say no. Tough or not, it is important to do so. Parents should try not to fall into what Nancy Samalin, Ph.D., author of *Loving Your Child Is Not Enough*, describes as the "Happiness Trap." In this situation, parents will buy or do anything just to keep their children happy and avoid their being angry at them. How can parents avoid this trap?

First, they may need to examine their own attitudes toward money and consider how these feelings are transferred to their children. If parents demonstrate responsibility by living within a budget, their children also are likely to be responsible with their money. In addition, parents need to understand how children of different ages perceive money and how to teach children about money.

Children can begin early to appreciate the fact that family resources are limited, that wishes sometimes conflict with financial realities, that hard choices have to be made, and that waiting is often necessary as money is saved to make a purchase. Children do not need to be "protected" from money worries, as some parents seem to feel. On the contrary, as Phyllis Theroux wrote in *Parents* magazine (April 1989), ". . . like sex, money is something children need to understand—not as an abstraction but as a reality that sooner rather than later will complicate their lives."

By the time they are three or four, children are generally ready to understand the basics of money. At this point, they know that parents give people in stores coins and bills and take home food and household items in return. However, they understand little about the value of money. For example, if given a choice of a nickel or a dime, they may be more likely to choose the nickel because it is the bigger coin. Young children can learn more about money by helping parents choose items in the grocery store, or by being told that they can pick out something that costs fifty cents or less. They also will enjoy playing with different kinds of coins and learning their names.

By the time they are in school, children can be encouraged to put coins in a piggy bank and should visit a real bank with a parent. Because they are learning numbers in school, they can begin counting coins and adding their values. They will also understand that a dime is worth more than a nickel. While shopping, they can learn to compare sizes of products with their prices.

To many parents, children between the ages of six and 10 seem overly preoccupied by money. Some may seem to talk about money constantly: what they would buy with it or what they want other people to buy for them. Parents may begin to worry that their children are on the road to becoming greedy adults. However, this phase is normal. Children are generally self-centered until they reach the age of nine or 10. They, like many adults, see money as a way to get what they want now, not as something to be saved and spent wisely. They also are greatly influenced by the instant gratification attitude of today's society. Money may seem magically powerful to them as well, because they do not understand where it comes from or the work parents do to earn it. It may be helpful for parents to talk about getting paid for work and how the money is used to pay for necessities, such as housing, food, and clothing, before it can be used for luxuries, such as toys and videos.

One of the most common ways to provide children with some understanding of money and some practice in using it is to give them a weekly allowance. The amount should be determined by family finances, community standards, and what the funds are expected to cover. All issues relating to the allowance should be openly discussed and agreed on so that they do not provide fodder for family battles. Questions to resolve include: What is the money to be used for? Can allowance money be spent freely or should a child be asked to account for it? Should a certain portion of an allowance be put aside as savings? Is a child expected to do chores in exchange for the allowance, or should chores and an allowance be kept as two separate issues? Should the allowance be given weekly, every two weeks, or monthly?

Harold and Sandy Moe, authors of *Teach Your Child the Value of Money*, recommend that a child be allowed to spend an allowance however he sees fit. Parents may offer guidance or advice in how to spend it, but the final decision should rest with the child. This may be hard at times. As one mother explained, ''We let Brian learn from his purchasing mistakes. Receiving a weekly allowance of a dollar, Brian finds it hard to save and is quick to spend it on small, cheap items that break easily or do not hold his interest. Slowly but surely, I believe he's making progress. After he passed up a recent purchase, he said, 'You know, my conscience told me I shouldn't buy that junk.' ''

At first a parent may be tempted to give a child more if he spends his allowance immediately and asks for an advance. Parents might allow this once, but they should try early on to keep within the set limits so that their children can learn to do the same.

If a child is eager to own something that his parents consider a luxury, they might help him plan the purchase rather than just buy what he asks for or refuse outright. Planning a purchase provides both a lesson in responsible saving and a demonstration that he has the power to achieve his goals. Parents might encourage the child to save part of his allowance in a piggy bank or a bank account as well as offer extra income possibilities in the form of jobs around the house, in addition to his regular chores. Parents may also offer to match any contributions he makes toward a purchase. This may depend on whether they consider the purchase worthwhile (such as a computer to use for schoolwork) or not (such as a trendy article of clothing).

One mother of a seven-year-old recalls the dilemma she faced when her son pleaded for Nintendo, the home video game that became wildly popular in the 1980s:

> *I was very reluctant to let Doug have the game, but it was just so important to him. He wanted nothing else. Finally, we agreed that if he saved up the cash from his allowance, he could buy it himself. Doug stopped buying his customary candy treats to save money and offered to do extra work around the house for cash. After three months, he was able to make the purchase. In the end, we were both satisfied. Although I still don't like the game, I was proud of his ability to save for what he wanted.*

As children begin to understand more about the value of money, they can also be encouraged to think of other people and to contribute some of their money to charity or other worthwhile causes.

Once children reach adolescence, they are capable of learning how to budget. At this point parents might want to share information about the running of the household on the income they make and the kinds of problems people often face trying to make ends meet. If parents feel that their child's spending habits are really irresponsible or out of control, they might help him write out a spending plan for a small amount of time, such as a week, so he has some idea where his money goes.

Many adolescents are eager to work for their own money. At its best a job provides worthwhile lessons in independence and responsibility. However, paid work also has a downside for teens. Work is time-consuming and may distract a child from academic or extracurricular pursuits. Moreover, since many kids are reluctant to save for long-term goals, such as going to college, their earnings often go for luxuries and the expenses of socializing. Sometimes it is even used to purchase alcohol or drugs. A further drawback when teens work is that there is less family time, and parents inevitably experience a certain loss of control.

To help a teenager get the most out of his work experience, parental supervision is important. If he has never had a bank account of his own, this is the time to suggest that he set one up. Parents also can discuss his long-range financial goals and suggest ways to achieve them. They may not expect him to contribute to the household budget, but they can certainly ask him to pay for more of his own clothes or school supplies. Above all, a teenager needs to know that his first responsibility is to complete his schoolwork. If his grades begin to suffer, the part-time job may have to go.

## Special Considerations for Adolescents

With persistence (and a little luck), the lessons learned in early childhood within the family about cooperation, communication, negotiation, and financial responsibility will carry through the adolescent years. Ideally the child who returns home at the appointed hour in his younger years, who is in the habit of talking about his activities, and who learns that Mom and Dad listen to him and support his drive toward maturity, will be the adolescent who respects his curfew and considers the family a safe environment in which to share confidences.

However, adolescence brings with it such enormous physiological, intellectual, and emotional changes that this model behavior is far from assured. "A burst of growth propels the adolescent toward the future," writes Louise J. Kaplan, Ph.D., in *Adolescence: The Farewell to Childhood.* In the process the adolescent begins to strain against the family ties he may feel constrict him. Suddenly the values painstakingly instilled in a child may seem to be dismissed as worthless. Where once his parents were the center of his universe, they may now be tyrants hobbled by hopelessly old-fashioned ideas. Parental restrictions no longer seem fair or reasonable, and efforts to communicate are now interpreted as insistent prying.

At its most strained, the parent-teen relationship can be marked by enormous conflicts. Threatened by a teen's rejection of time-honored family values, parents may tighten their grip in a final determined effort to retain control of their child. A teen may respond with a ferocious effort to break free of constrictions. If the lines of conflict harden, it can be a long time before a truce can be negotiated. In the meantime parents may also give up trying and retreat, despairing of ever again having a decent relationship with their child.

Pitched battles or stony silences need not be an inevitable part of family life with an adolescent, however. Although teens may balk at parental efforts to restrict them, they do not want to discard completely the security of their pasts. To understand the mixed signals they get from their teenagers, who may be defiant one minute, sad the next, and cheerful and affectionate after that, parents have to listen carefully and read between the lines. What parents don't see—a young person who might actually be listening and who doesn't really want to cause so much turmoil—they may have to take on faith. What they should remember is that no matter how independent a teenager may appear, he still needs parental guidance, love, support, and limits to help him deal with a confusing, conflicting world in which he is trying to find a comfortable place.

How parents set the stage for rule-making plays a major part in a teen's perception of the fairness of rules and whether or not he complies with them. Restrictions, writes Dr. Haim G. Ginott in *Between Parent and Teenager*, should not be imposed in a spirit of anger and argument, nor in a language that invites resistance. They also should not be established on a whim without reason behind them. It is better instead that "limits are set in a manner that preserves our teenagers' self-respect. The limits are neither arbitrary nor capricious. They are anchored in values and aimed at character-building."

Teenagers usually appreciate straight, honest talk that doesn't resort to accusations and threats. Parents need to state clearly how they feel and give some explanation of why they're worried or upset or unwilling to compromise. They also need to listen respectfully to their child's point of view and consider where they might give a little without giving in. For example, a young teenager who refuses to attend a religious service with his family might be willing to go if he is allowed to attend services by himself. Parents must realize, however, that forcing this and certain other activities on older teens is fruitless.

Teenagers also need to practice making their own decisions and exercising good judgment, based on a consideration of consequences and others' feelings. Fourteen-year-old Hanna remarked, "I just want Mom to trust me. I don't go with the fast crowd, I'm not interested in drinking, and I get my schoolwork done. But I'm old enough to go downtown by myself and I don't want to have to call home every 15 minutes just to say I'm safe." Although Hanna may be demonstrably trustworthy enough to forgo frequent calling, she has not considered her mother's justified worries about her safety. She also has not considered that someone does need to know where she is, just in case something does happen. The solution may be a rule stating that she call home only once during the evening or if she decides to go somewhere other than her originally planned destination.

Teenagers should be reminded that there are legal and social rules, as well as family rules, which responsible people must follow to keep life bearable for everyone. Shoplifting, using illicit drugs, drinking under the legal age, driving recklessly—these things are against the civil law as well as the family's rules. Parents need to be clear that these behaviors will not be tolerated. Parents also should call on professional help when needed.

Most parents want their children to become confident and independent, and to do so responsibly. Teenagers who are struggling to grow up will come to realize that life is easier when lived in a spirit of cooperation and honest communication. Parents who are patient will find that in time teens will come to appreciate their family once again. Then they will be secure that they have a solid base from which to face the outside world.

● ● ● ● ● ● ● ● ● ● ● ● ● ● ● ● ● ● ● ● ● ● ● ● ● ● ● ● ● ● ● ● ● ● ● ● ● ●

## Parents ask:

*Out of necessity, my 10-year-old daughter has to baby-sit for her six-year-old sister every day after school until I'm home from work. Her teacher says that she's the most grown-up kid she's ever met. I worry, though, that I'm asking too much of her. Am I?*

Reality sometimes makes certain demands on parents and children that are not pleasant. If an economic situation means that a parent has no alternative but to ask his child to take care of a younger sibling, then that parent should not be made to feel guilty about this necessity. The problem, however, is not having to take care of a younger sibling. It's the monotony of doing so every day. The situation can be made more palatable by spreading out the responsibility. The parent might allow the older child to invite a friend over on some afternoons so they can baby-sit together. He might also arrange occasional afternoons for the younger sister to stay with a relative or have a playdate at the home of her friends, giving the older sister some time for herself. By being more flexible and inventive, this parent can turn a difficult situation into an enriching experience.

# CHAPTER FOUR

· · · · · ·

# Friendships and Peer Groups

**A** friend is many things to different people. Writing in *Fruits of Solitude*, the early American William Penn defined a true friend as one who "advises justly, assists readily, adventures boldly, takes all patiently, defends courageously," while psychologist Laurence J. Peter, Ed.D., author of *The Peter Principle*, says, "You can always tell a real friend: when you've made a fool of yourself he doesn't feel you've done a permanent job." Adults generally insist on some sort of give-and-take from a friend. To a toddler, a friend might be any other child she sees who is her size and who is willing to play the same games she is playing. An eight-year-old child may see a friend as the one she not only spends time with but to whom she has pledged loyalty and vice versa, even though they may argue often over small issues. A 12-year-old may describe a friend as someone with whom she can share secrets, someone she can talk to for hours on the telephone. While many people, young or old, may have different ideas about what a friend should be, most agree that friends are important.

Friends are the first personal contacts with the world outside of the family. The continuing relationships with friends through the years serve as an important foundation for children's future success in the many social interactions that form a life. In *Children's Friendships*, Zick Rubin, Ph.D., writes, "Friends serve central functions for children that parents do not, and they play a critical role in shaping children's social skills and their sense of identity. Children's experiences with their friends may also have major effects on their later development, including their orientations toward friendship and love as adults.''

Dr. Rubin further states that childhood friendships are important because they provide opportunities for learning how to share, communicate, and empathize with others. Through friendships children are exposed to a wide range of social situations in which they must ask for what they need from each other and learn how to negotiate. For example, a child learns how to ask (''I'll let you use my shovel if I can borrow your dump truck'') and how to suggest (''Would you like to try putting my shovel and your dump truck together to see what we can make?'').

Childhood friendships encourage the development of a sense of identity. For example, when children say to each other, ''I can run faster than you,'' parents might worry that their children are becoming too competitive. However, such conversations help children recognize their own distinct physical characteristics and personality traits.

Friendships also foster a sense of belonging. Identifying with a peer group can give a child security and a sense of her place in the world as she gains confidence in her own independence. In addition to the developmental advantages, friendships also add immeasurably to the joy of being a human. Sharing the world with a companion who is also seeing it for the first time makes growing up a lot more fun.

## The Responsibilities of Being a Friend

Having friends brings rich rewards and personal satisfaction. However, keeping friendships alive and healthy is also a responsibility for everyone involved, as the nineteenth-century philosopher Ralph Waldo Emerson expressed in his essay "Friendship": "The only way to have a friend is to be one." As a young child begins to experience the fun of having friendships, parents can point out what it means to be a friend, primarily by demonstrating caring behavior with their own friends. Dr. Elaine Heffner writes in *Mothering*:

> *In the development of social behavior, the major task is to grow from a position where one demands total attention for one's own needs and feelings to the point of being able to give consideration to the needs and feelings of others. The objective is some balance between self and others. The challenge for child rearing is to help a child move from one position to the other in such a way that he does not come to believe that his own needs and feelings are wrong, and must be sacrificed for someone else, or that others must be made to sacrifice their needs and feelings for him.*

Finding this balance can be a complicated process. Parents can certainly tell their children what being a good friend means:

- Friendship is mutual. It should not be formed merely for convenience or personal gain.
- Friends are loyal and reliable. They stand by each other, whether or not one person becomes more popular, is accepted by a clique, or gains recognition for her athletic or academic accomplishments. Friends also keep commitments, even if a more tempting offer comes along.
- Friends keep each other's trust. Gossiping, spreading rumors, or teasing a friend publicly about something shared in private is not acceptable behavior.
- Friends are emotionally supportive. They cheer each oth-

er's successes and provide comfort when one is sad or upset. They also support each other's goals unless a goal becomes self-destructive or harmful to other people, in which case a friend helps her friend get help.

- Friends are able to communicate openly, expressing their needs without hurting each other's feelings. They also respect each other's differences.
- Friends are not possessive of each other.

Of course, children often have a hard time being the kind of friends they should be. Kids (and grown-ups, too) do form friendships for personal gain, they do gossip about friends, they are not always open with each other, and they do hurt each other's feelings. Sometimes all parents can do is to help their children survive and understand the hurts, disappointments, and jealousies they will inevitably experience, as well as learn from their mistakes. Parents also need to remind themselves that these ups and down are a normal part of growing up.

## The Evolving Pattern of Children's Friendships

By the time children reach the age of two or three, they have established their first bonds with each other. As they explore the world beyond the boundaries of family over the next several years, these peer relationships become ever more important.

First friendships are usually formed with children who live near each other, who take part in the same day-care program or play group, or who are children of parents' friends. Even though young children may not be able to tell why they like another child, they may talk to their parents about friends, ask when they can play together again, and get excited when plans are made to meet. These first attachments are important. Children may not have a fully developed sense of loyalty to or sharing with a friend, but they can show a preference for being with particular children.

Parents can encourage the development of these budding friendships by arranging time for children to be together and by being sensitive to their child's possible sadness when a friend moves away. They can also use their child's desire to be with other children to help her learn how to care about other people's feelings. For example, a parent might tell a child that by learning to share toys and not hitting when she's angry, other children will be more likely to want to be her friend.

Around the age of five and into the early school years, many children experience jealousy and a sense of rivalry with their friends. They may become upset that a friend has more of something, such as ice cream, toys, or the attention of an adult, just as they might become jealous of a sibling. Young school-age friends may argue over rules and about what others are "supposed" to do. They are heavily involved in what is fair or not fair, usually in terms of how it affects them personally. This may lead to fights with friends that are often over just as quickly as they begin. Even though children of this age disagree with one another, they hold onto their friendships. They can feel loyal toward one or more friends, a feeling that intensifies when they enter school and become a part of a distinct group. This loyalty can, at times, result in children's harsh treatment of one another. Friends may join together to tease or bully another child. A child may also become angry at another child because she perceives that the child has hurt a friend.

Parents remain a central part of their child's life at this

**103**

stage, modeling values and providing a safe haven against sometimes harsh peer interactions. They can best help the child develop friendships by stressing the importance of cooperation and consideration of others' feelings. They also can help their child see how her actions affect others. When the child begins to see herself defined in part by the reactions of others to her, she gets a better sense of who she is as a person outside the family.

Peer acceptance assumes its greatest importance to children between the ages of about nine and 12. At this time cliques begin to form and "best friends" become crucial. Many children grow terribly fearful of not fitting in or of being labeled "different." They may constantly compare their appearance, attitudes, and family life with what they see in other children and end up criticizing themselves for not measuring up to the group's standard. Young girls in particular like to dress in the same manner as one another and to wear their hair in the same style. Everyone wants to see the same movies, have as many privileges as they perceive their friends to have, and own whatever toy or item of clothing is currently in vogue.

In the middle and late teenage years, children gradually develop a clearer sense of personal identity and an appreciation for the value of individualism. Ironically, that sense of individualism is found in a group, and teens rely more than ever on friends for sharing their confidences and talking about feelings. Although parents often feel shut out of a teenager's life at this stage ("Tiffany can spend hours whispering to friends in her room, but she just clams up at the dinner table"), this behavior is not only typical but also important to the child's development. Most teenagers will still want to talk with parents, especially when something is really troubling them, but the times for talking openly with parents probably will be sporadic.

Even though teenagers begin to think carefully about

themselves in relation to others and start to ask themselves profound questions, they may find it difficult to be open even with friends about their deepest personal worries and fears. In *The Moral Life of Children*, psychiatrist Robert Coles, M.D., describes a free-form dialogue with four high school students, in which the students grappled earnestly with moral issues:

> *The tension between loyalty to one's friends and loyalty to one's own memories, habits, yearnings; the tension between one's competitive side and one's regard for others; the tension between one's wish to win and one's willingness to help others. The word "honesty" was mentioned over and over—who is "really" honest, and for what "underlying" reasons? Moreover, does it "pay" in this society to be honest all the time? When does pride in one's convictions turn into bullying egotism? If you really do have a "sense of yourself," are you not in danger of being smug and self-serving? When does popularity reduce one's individuality to the point of belonging only to the herd?*

Although resolving the issues that the teens discussed may take each of them a lifetime of searching, the fact that the issues were even raised reflects the teenagers' growing maturity and a significant change in the way they begin to think about themselves, their friends, and their world.

## The Promise and the Peril of Peer Groups

Peer groups offer a mirror in which a child can see her own reflection. By helping her to secure a safe place away from home, a peer group can also provide stability, ease the process of separation from family, and create a foundation for achievement in the larger world. At their worst, peer groups can be a source of pressure, encouraging a child to act in inappropriate ways or to indulge in risky behavior in order to feel accepted. Behavior that a child may feel forced into adopting can include cruelly treating other children not considered a part of the group, dating and becoming sexually intimate, experimenting with drugs and/or alcohol, destroying property, or stealing. Standing up to such peer pressure takes a great deal of courage and a well-developed sense of self-esteem at an age when such confidence is often at a low point. It also takes parents who continue to be there for their teenager even when the child seems to be pushing them away.

Most often peer group influences are relatively benign and fall between the extremes of being profoundly good or profoundly bad influences on kids. Typically, peer pressure focuses on outward appearances, entertainment choices, participation in after-school activities, and choices of friends. Child development experts recognize that conformity is part of the normal growth pattern and that it allows a child to come to grips with social influences. Parents can take comfort in knowing that, over time, a more mature balance between group norms and individual preferences will develop. In one study entitled "Conformity as a Function of Age," child psychologists P. R. Constanzo and M. E. Shaw charted the power of group influence as a function of age. Their graph showed that the inclination to conform rises within the seven- to nine-year-old age group, peaks among 11- to 13-year-olds, and falls away steadily afterwards. Nonetheless, peer groups remain highly influential all through the teenage years.

A productive peer group ideally is one that claims to be different from other groups rather than better or worse than those outside the group. A productive peer group also goes beyond a single set of standards or activities, and encourages diversity and independence. Parents should not worry if their children's peer groups do not attain these ideals; most groups don't. But parents need not be passive bystanders, either. With an attitude of respect toward their child, parents can try to remind her of the ideals toward which a group should strive. For example, if a parent is concerned about the rejection of another child by the peer group, the parent might say, "Why don't you invite Cory to go to the mall with your friends? Remember when we first moved to this town and you felt so good when Jennifer asked you to tag along with her and her friends?" If the child stubbornly rejects such a suggestion, a parent might instead state outright what her feelings are while still recognizing her child's ability to make a choice ("It's your group and you make your own rules and decisions, but I think you should invite Cory"). The difference in approach may seem small, but a child may not be so quick to reject a suggestion that is left up to her.

In addition, parents may help children of any age retain a sense of priorities. As a result, children will be able to gain the benefits of healthy peer interaction without being subject to undue pressures. There is nothing unusual about a child who wants to dress the way her peers do or go to the "in" movies. On the other hand, if she's caught shoplifting "because everyone else was doing it," or collared in the act of uprooting Mrs. Smith's rosebush "because the kids called me a coward when I said I didn't want to," then there's a problem that needs to be dealt with promptly.

Parents also should respect a child's right to make her own decisions. It is hard to overestimate how important wearing the appropriate clothes, being chosen for the right sports team, or even carrying the proper type of book bag can be to a child. Obviously not much can be done about a child's appearance ("Can I bleach out my freckles, Mom?"), and parents have every right to hold firm against drastic or dangerous attempts to change it. But if no harm comes from a child's preferences, even if parents think that wearing mismatched socks or cutoff sweatpants worn under shorts looks absurd, it is best to accommodate them. These are ways children are trying to distinguish themselves from the adult world and make what they do and say important to them.

A child needs to know that her parents are her allies. When peer pressures intensify, she needs to feel that she is protected from the temptations of risky behavior. Whether the issue is skipping school, going to a party where older kids are likely to be drinking, or accepting a date with an older youngster, firm enforcement of family rules helps fortify a child against negative influences. It also can give a child a ready excuse to fall back on if she feels she isn't strong enough to say no herself ("I'd love to go, but my mom would kill me").

Listening empathetically while children talk about their experiences with friends and helping them clarify their feelings about a situation, whether good or bad, keeps everyone attuned to the impact of peer relationships. Communication will also allow parents to help their children decide what they might want to do in a situation. For example, Wendy suddenly announced to her parents that she didn't want to be on the track team in school. Since she had enjoyed the team so much, Wendy's parents asked her why she had suddenly changed her mind. They found out that Wendy still enjoyed track but had been told by her friends that track wasn't "cool" and would cut into their time hanging out together. Wendy's parents helped her decide what *she* most wanted to do, rather than allow herself to be swayed by the opinions of others.

Parents should also encourage their children to participate in adult-run peer groups, such as scouting or a swim team, in addition to their participation in child-run peer groups. Adult-run peer groups give children experience with groups that have clearly stated ideals and goals.

## On Childhood Cruelty

In their effort to fit in with one group of kids, children can go to extremes to exclude or badger another child. There are endless examples. During the first years of school, a group of kids may gang up to tease another child, ridicule a new kid on the block, or refuse to invite someone to a birthday party. As cliques form in the preadolescent years, an unfortunate subset of kids is often designated as "outcasts" to be scorned and rejected by the "in" crowd. By junior high school a host of personality types, including "nerds," "jocks," "grinds," and "fast girls," have been classified according to a hierarchy of acceptability only an adolescent can fully understand. Despite the commonality of such behavior, parents need to take a prompt and firm stand against displays of cruel behavior. While they can't control their kids' actions all the time, declaring cruelty unacceptable is an important first step toward checking it. Parents who shrug off mean behavior as an inevitable part of childhood allow the community of children to operate with no control and encourage future adults to have little empathy toward others. How can parents help set the standards by which they want their kids to live? Some suggestions:

- **Encourage children to respect differences among their peers, not to mock them.** Children who are considered different because of the way they look, the activities they enjoy, or their family background are frequently subject to taunts and ridicule from their peers. Teaching a child to tolerate difference is a paramount parental responsibility. One parent who overheard her eight-year-old son make the remark ''David isn't good because he doesn't go to church on Sunday'' responded, ''David doesn't go to church on Sunday because his family is Jewish. Saturday is the day of worship for Jews. Before you criticize his beliefs, find out more about them. Perhaps he wouldn't mind taking you to synagogue with him someday so you could see what the services are like.''

If a parent hears a child cruelly mimic another child's accent or traditions, she could say, ''Maria speaks with an accent because she comes from Mexico. I think it would be fun to learn something about another country. We could probably learn a lot from her. Would you like to ask her over for lunch sometime and we could get to know her better?''

The dangers of labeling should also be conveyed, especially in light of the fact that they can be untrue as well as damaging. Parents can point out that people's talents can shine in different situations. A boy who has been labeled a ''nerd'' in a sports-oriented school because of his interest in science and mathematics might be considered a real star in computer camp. A girl who is considered ''dumb'' academically might have an exceptional talent in sports or art. Parents also should be aware of how they themselves might label other individuals and groups, which encourages their children to do the same.

- **Provide support in meeting the challenge of being different.** A child needs to learn not only how to be tolerant of others who are different but how to deal with others who might label *her* as different. A kid who is criticized by friends for getting good grades or wanting to pursue an interest that isn't considered popular needs parental support. Parents can help their child sort out her feelings about what she really wants to do vs. what her friends want her to do. Although it may be a small comfort at the time, parents can remind a preteen or teenager that popularity is fleeting and that the most popular young people in high school are often not those who are the greatest successes later in life. Parents also can help a child try to focus on her future goals. A child can be encouraged to think about whether or not turning from her goals and dreams in order to gain a possibly short-lived acceptance from a few friends is worth it. Rather than insist that their child give up peers, however, parents can help steer her to groups that will help, not hinder, her development.

Accepting the fact of physical or developmental disability can be particularly challenging both for the child who has special health needs and for the nondisabled child. Meeting the problem head-on often decreases the discomfort on both sides. Parents of disabled children and parents of nondisabled kids need to help their children discover that a disabled person is still a person in every way.

The following is an example of how this approach might work: When 10-year-old Annie developed an unusual blood sugar problem, her doctor insisted that she follow a special diet. That meant that Annie had to carry her lunch from home instead of buying it at the school cafeteria like most of the other kids. She also had to skip the midafternoon class snack. Annie's mother thought carefully about how to win her daughter's cooperation without making her feel conspicuous. She began encouraging Annie to take part in their search for a solution. Together they decided to pack a brightly decorated goody box with her special foods. To Annie's delight, all the kids began clamoring for their own goody boxes!

Suppose Annie's mother had instead adopted a moralistic stance that said in essence, "Well, it's too bad but she'll just have to learn to accept this." Whether or not Annie actually ate the recommended foods, there is little doubt that she would have done so reluctantly, rather than enthusiastically.

- **Provide emotional support to children who have trouble making friends.** Parents are naturally concerned if their child is a loner or seems unable to sustain a friendship over a long period of time. They may also be tempted to step in and try to fix the problem or push their child into activities she doesn't want to do. Parents need to remember that children must learn to fight their own battles if they are to develop proper social skills. Expressing pity ("Poor Dana, the other kids are really mean to you, aren't they?") accomplishes little more than making a child overly dependent. It is better to make concrete suggestions and help the child work through the problem for herself. ("Why do you think the children were mean to you? They might not have let you play because they already had enough players by the time you got there. What do you think you could say or do to help them get to know you better? Perhaps you would like to invite one of them over later.") All a child needs to get started is one friend, and almost every child finds one eventually with encouragement—but without pushing—from a parent.

## Bullying

A child who is the victim of bullying by her peers needs both protection and an ego boost, as well as some specific help. It's important not to blame the victim. Statements such as "If you didn't look so scared maybe the kids would leave you alone" or "Act nicer and the other kids will treat you better" burden a child with unfair responsibility for her own misery. Instead parents should concentrate on helping the victim of a bully recognize that she is not at fault because of someone else's cruelty. This may be an appropriate time for parents to remind their child that other people are not always as supportive as they should be.

Talking candidly with a child about the problem may also help. Parents can remind her that hurtful verbal assaults should be ignored. They should, however, acknowledge her genuine pain, ("I know it hurts to be called names. But you and I know you're not a crybaby, no matter what Max says.") Try to help a child understand the situation. Asking "Why do you think Max teases you?" may bring recognition that Max is insecure and needs to show off to get attention.

A child also needs some ideas for protecting herself against the bullying. Since most parents do not want their child to respond to verbal abuse or even physical attacks with violence, a child first should be encouraged to seek help from an adult, such as a teacher. The child may worry that friends will accuse her of being cowardly or of tattling, but she can be assured that her peers are likely to respect her if she makes it clear to a bully that she is going to an authority because she does not believe in fighting and will not be pushed around. For example, a child might say, "It's dumb for us to fight over this. If you keep trying to hit me, I'm going to get the teacher to stop you." The bully most likely has been bothering other children as well, so the one child who takes action will probably gain support from other kids.

If a child can get no help from an authority, either because a teacher or a counselor is not available or is ineffective, parents might consider teaching her how to defend herself, emphasizing that the best defense is to get away from potential harm. A child's self-esteem can be helped, however, by learning that she can physically defend herself if need be. Dr. Thomas Lickona in *Raising Good Children* writes, ''At the very least, learning self-defense is a confidence-builder. Kids who feel they can handle themselves don't send out the 'vulnerability signals' that make some children prone to attack.''

If a bully is much older and stronger than her victim, the parents may need to intervene. This may mean talking to the bully or to the aggressive child's parents. In this situation, Dr. Lickona recommends that parents ''step out of the middle as soon as you can and let your child speak for himself. That's good experience for him (or her), and it's easier for the other parent to hear the story from your child. If you don't get satisfactory results on the phone, ask if you can come over with your child. Confronted with his victim under such circumstances, the bullying child will have a hard time telling a plausible lie. Even if he still doesn't own up to his actions, chances are he's not going to want to face this kind of a scene again, and the terrorizing of your child will stop.''

If parents discover that their child is the aggressor rather than the victim, it's important to examine the reasons for her aggressive behavior. Sometimes the child merely lacks social graces and needs practice and encouragement to behave more appropriately. Sometimes a pattern of hostile behavior masks frustration, stress, or difficulties in communicating with others. She may also be experiencing anger at a particular situation, such as an imagined slight from other children, or an upset with a teacher or parent. She may also have an undeveloped sense of the harm she is causing others. Unless parents deal with the real reasons their child needs to bully, her behavior problems are likely to worsen over time.

Once a child has been pegged as a bully, her problems

multiply as she continues to have difficulty making friends, thus fueling her anger and resentment.

## Shifting Allegiances and Broken Friendships

Early friendships are frequently unstable; old bonds are broken and new alliances are forged frequently during the life of almost every child. At points of transition, such as graduating from elementary or junior high school, moving to a different neighborhood, or joining a new club, it is particularly common for friends to drift apart. Changing interests also lead to both the gain and loss of friendships.

In their younger years children have curious notions about loyalty. For example, Toby and Steven, both six, are next-door neighbors and best friends. But Toby also has a good friend named Jaime from his after-school program, and on some Saturdays Toby and Jaime meet to play at Toby's house. One Saturday, Steven wandered next door for a visit and was told in no uncertain terms, "You can't come over today. My friend Jaime is here and we are playing together." On another occasion when Steven came by, however, Toby left Jaime in the lurch, telling him, "You have to go home now. I want to play with Steven."

In part, this scenario reflects the fact that young children are often unskilled at playing in groups larger than two. Their allegiances also change regularly, as is illustrated by the revolving door through which even "best friends" are often sent:

"I don't like Jane any more," complains an eight-year-old girl.

"Last week you told me she was your best friend," Mom
points out.

"I know. But now she ignores me and plays with Jennifer
instead. Sonia is my best friend now."

In *Children's Frienships*, Dr. Zick Rubin writes, "The end-
ings of friendships and their replacement with new ones
should usually be taken as signs of normal development
rather than of social inadequacy." Nonetheless, lost friendship can be quite stressful to a child, and parents need to
empathize with their child's feelings rather than dismissing
them. While youngsters usually bounce back and move
ahead to make new friends, it is common for at least one
child to feel rejected and hurt when relationships end.

Adolescents generally assume more responsibility for
maintaining friendships. Nonetheless, differing levels of
maturity, changing interests, and the relative importance a
preteen or teen assigns to her academic, sports, and social
activities combine to keep social connections in flux. Writes
Dr. Rubin: "Assessments of the cause of a breakup play a
critical role in determining one's reaction to it. Whereas self-
blame, for example, may discourage children from attempting to form new friendships (on the ground that 'no one
could ever like me'), a fuller understanding of the psychological differences that led to a breakup can help them to
establish more satisfactory friendships in the future." Parents may help children reach an understanding of a lost
friendship by reassuring them that friends often grow apart
because their interests and goals changed and not because
of any mistake they committed or any personal failing.
Some children, however, *may* need to be made aware that
their own disregard for another's feelings caused the
breakup of a friendship.

With help from adults it is sometimes possible to repair

damaged friendships. Lorraine Joy Weber, a human resource facilitator at the White Plains Intermediate School in
Westchester, New York, often deals with broken friendships among the 10-, 11-, and 12-year-olds she counsels. To
help warring children work through their differences, Ms.
Weber will physically position them in chairs at opposite
ends of the room and say, ''I know that you are really this
far apart right now, but I would like you to both think about
something positive that happened between you in the
past.'' As they remember good times, she encourages each
child to move her chair a bit closer. When they are close
together again, Ms. Weber says, ''You see, you have
choices. In relationships you can move closer or you can
move further apart. It is up to you to choose.'' Her objective is not to insist that they repair a damaged friendship
but to remind them that differences can be bridged if both
parties are willing to assume the responsibility of trying.

Parents, too, can help children patch up differences between friends. With young children, parents may need to
intervene and ask children to talk about why they are angry
with each other and what they could do to be friends again.
With older children, parents might first talk to their child
about why she thinks the conflict occurred, in the hope of
getting to the root of the problem. For example, Roy became very angry at his friend David for criticizing the way
he threw a baseball. Roy claimed that David knew nothing
about baseball and had no right to say anything. Roy's father discovered that Roy was actually hurt because David had
criticized him in front of other boys and had been, what Roy
called, showing off. Roy still wanted to be friends with David,
but he wanted him to know how he felt. Roy's father suggested
that Roy call David on the phone and talk about the argument
or invite him over. His father offered to stay around the house
while the boys talked, in case Roy needed him.

# Parents as Role Models

While watching their children navigate the complexities of human relationships, parents should not underestimate their own influence. Through modeling appropriate relationships, discouraging irresponsible behavior, and respecting the limits of a child's sociability, parents can play a major part in teaching their children to appreciate the richness of friendship. The depth and breadth of parents' own friendships communicate the message that they value positive connections with other people.

Sometimes, however, in remembering their own childhood, parents push their children to "fit in" or overemphasize the need to belong or be liked by others. Diane, the mother of four girls between the ages of two and 10, still remembers how her schoolmates made fun of her for being overweight. "I hated being called Two-Ton Tillie and having to wear chubette dresses. I always made good grades, but who cared? I was embarrassed to try to do anything else. That experience has left me with a lifelong determination to keep my children from feeling like misfits. I really want them to be popular and to feel that they belong."

It's important to remember that children, like adults, differ greatly in their need for friendships. While all children should have the confidence and self-esteem to relate comfortably to their peers, not everyone needs to be surrounded by a circle of friends at all times. Many children delight in time spent reading or playing alone. The mother of two daughters, ages 11 and nine, remembers: "Molly never felt happy unless there were other kids around to play with, but Alice was content to play by herself for hours at a time." Whatever the blend of genetic and environmental influences that make up a child's personality, her social needs are highly individualistic and should be respected.

## When Parents Don't Like Their Child's Friends

What if parents are unhappy with their child's choice of friends? "It takes a delicate system of checks and balances to allow a child the responsibility of choosing his own friends while we keep the responsibility of ensuring that the choice is a beneficial one," wrote Dr. Haim G. Ginott in *Between Parent and Child.* Often, a hands-off approach that demonstrates respect for a child's judgment and autonomy is the best course of action. A child with a healthy self-esteem and with self-confidence may occasionally strike up a friendship that parents don't approve of, but most likely it will run its course without doing her any harm.

Parents also may need to consider *why* they don't like a child's friend. The other child may exhibit traits that parents would find annoying in friends of their own, but parents need to remember that their child is an individual person who may value a friend for reasons parents can't see. Parents might reserve their judgment by reminding themselves that their child's friend is also going through the ups and downs of growing up, and most children go through stages that are annoying to adults but are acceptable to other children. Once parents get to know each of their child's friends a bit better, they may find qualities they enjoy that will help them overlook what they don't like.

If parents are convinced that their child's friend is a bad influence, more aggressive intervention may be appropriate. Before taking action, however, parents need to remember that discouraging counterproductive friendships is a delicate matter. It's usually best not to bar a child from seeing a friend altogether. Most likely they will see each other in school or during after-school activities anyway. Forbidding a friendship may only make it more enticing. Subtler tactics generally are more effective.

For one thing, parents might impose restrictions in their

home and explain them clearly to their child. (''When you and Roger play together you always end up hitting your little brother. You know that is not allowed here. If you can't control your behavior when you are together, Roger will not be permitted to play in our home.'')

Helping to channel their child's energy into constructive activities, providing attentive supervision, and encouraging open communication are also elements parents might try in the struggle to overcome negative peer influences. One father shared his solution to a potentially problematic situation:

*We had allowed our eight-year-old son to play at a neighbor's house with their 11-year-old son because there were few other children on the block. After the couple divorced, we discovered that the neighbor was leaving his son home alone before and after school when he went to work. The boy had no supervision. Once he encouraged our son to go wandering around the neighborhood with him after we had called and told him to come straight home because it was getting dark. Then we found out quite by accident that he had been showing our son how to draw what we considered to be pornographic pictures of men and women. We had a long talk with our son about why the pictures were bad and what a loving relationship was between a man and a woman. We also talked to the other boy and his father. We didn't get much response from the father, so we forbade our son to play with the other boy alone. We knew it would be hard to keep them apart, so we told them they could play only at our house or in our yard when someone was home. We also made a point of talking with our son about his friend's situation and how the lack of adult supervision made it easy for him to get into trouble. We pointed out that even if our son behaved himself, his association with someone who misbehaved could also get him into trouble and cause others to think of him as a troublemaker.*

Kids can learn how to step away from trouble, too. Marty, age eight, lives in a small town north of San Francisco. He and his friends ride through the neighborhood on their bicycles and are allowed to be away from the house for two hours at a time. Marty has been given one firm rule: If one of his friends does something or intends to do something he knows is wrong, he is expected to leave the scene.

The rule originated with an incident a few years earlier. At the time, Marty was playing with a six-year-old boy near the latticework fence surrounding the home of an elderly couple. The younger boy began to break off pieces of the fence and construct a miniature fort with them. Although Marty didn't participate in this mischief, he was in as much trouble as his friend when the couple came home and discovered the damage. "He whined to us that he hadn't done it," Marty's father explained. "But we told him that standing there watching his friend misbehave was unacceptable even if he wasn't doing anything wrong. He felt that he had been punished unjustly, but it helped him see that if he doesn't walk away from someone else's misbehavior, he might be blamed for it."

This policy establishes an important precedent for the teenage years, when children are often exposed to riskier forms of misbehavior. Says 15-year-old Jennifer: "I have friends who like to party and that's fine, but they know I don't want to come along. If I go to a party and there are a lot of kids smoking and drinking, I'll just leave. I don't need to be a part of that."

A child who is continually attracted to friends her parents don't trust may have unresolved psychological conflicts that require further attention. Does she lack the confidence to assert herself within a group? Is she trying to prove that she is tough or daring, either to parents or to her peers? Is she venting unresolved anger through her self-destructive behavior? Is she looking for a way to assert her independence from an authoritarian family? Unraveling the root causes of a child's damaging relationships is usually the wisest way to cope with them.

## Bucking the Trend: Community Standards vs. Personal Values

In the context of peer relationships, a conflict between community standards and personal values sometimes arises. Barring a child from doing something all the other kids get to do is difficult for parent and child alike. The usual response is "It's not fair." Yet exercising judgment about a child's safety and enforcing reasonable restrictions are prime parental obligations. And while parents need to be flexible (they may want to think carefully about their rules if all the other kids really *are* doing something), they do have a right to try to preserve the values they have established for themselves and their families.

Julia's story reflects some of these conflicts. She decided to bar her 12-year-old son from seeing a popular, though violent, movie. To minimize his protests, she tried to persuade other parents to declare the film off-limits, but her efforts proved fruitless. Over and over she was told, "I'm going to let my child go because all his friends are going and he'll be upset if he is left out."

"I feel as if I'm always bucking the tide in my community," sighed Julia, adding that her experience suggests that parents find it easier to give in than to fight. "A lot of adults just don't want to take the responsibility of being parents." While that's a harsh and perhaps an unfair judgment, Julia's situation highlights the challenge of defining independent values rather than living by the norms of others. After continued persistence on her son's part, Julia finally offered him a compromise: He could see the movie if they went together and then had a talk about it afterward. Her son reluctantly agreed (part of the fun would have been seeing it with his friends). Later, Julia asked him why he liked the movie, why he thought the filmmaker had to show so much violence, what he thought of the characters who were hurt and killed, and if he could imagine his reaction had he witnessed something like that in real life. Then she told him her opinion. Julia managed to take away a lot of the movie's mystique and helped her son see it from a different perspective.

Paul tells a similar story about his seven-year-old daughter, who was instructed to play with her friends in the yard and sidewalk, not on the street. Initially her friends adhered to this restriction, but over time they decided it was more fun to ride their bikes into the street. Concerned about the danger, Paul began calling the other parents on the block and found that none of them were happy about bike riding in the street. However, no one wanted to enforce the restriction and have to deal with the reaction of their children. Paul finally found one parental ally, and together they found other activities for their children farther away from the street. Sometimes Paul feels that his restrictions keep his daughter on the sidelines of having fun with all the neighborhood children. "I don't want her to feel left out, but I'm not willing to jeopardize her safety," he says.

When parents convey to their child that she will not be allowed to do something no matter how many of her friends are doing it, they may be able to help her think of ways to approach her peers. These ways might include presenting a strong viewpoint that shows she has a mind of her own or having her use parental disapproval as a backup excuse to her friends.

Given life's daily pressures, parents need to pick their battles, standing firm only on the ones that really matter. But the responsibility for setting reasonable standards and defining limits is not one parents can afford to deny, even when it means the short-term loss of their children's approval. By holding the line, parents show their children that people can stand firm. This encourages kids to do the same as they move into the wider world of friends, school, and community.

• • • • • • • • • • • • • • • • • • • • • • • • • • • • • • •

## Parents ask:

*Up until last month, I always trusted my 14-year-old daugh-
ter. Then I caught her in a lie. I found out that she'd been
hanging out at the mall with some friends instead of being
at basketball practice, where she said she'd been. Now I feel
that I can't trust her at all. How can I trust her again?*

What's amazing is that this kid's first lie occurred at the age
of 14, since almost all children lie to their parents at some
point. This does not mean that they're beyond trust, nor
are they irresponsible. Because the parent in this situation
feels so badly, he needs to find some way to give his daughter a chance to earn his trust again. He can first let his
daughter know the consequence of her action. For example,
this may entail grounding her for a certain length of time
(or anything else that seems appropriate). He also can tell
his daughter that he is having trouble trusting her and can
ask her what she thinks she can do to earn his trust once
again. One example might be requiring her to call him
whenever she is out to let him know where she is or having
her come home at a certain time. Restrictions can be slowly
lifted as the parent feels more trusting. Lying is wrong, of
course, but should be expected. And there's always a way
for parents to regain trust in their child.

# CHAPTER FIVE

• • • • • •

# The School Years

**B**ecoming a student for the first time in the community school has long been the symbolic point at which a child takes his first steps away from the family and into a larger world. Although the experiences of day care and pre-school have blurred the impact of this symbol for many of today's children, formal entry into kindergarten or the first grade is still considered by many parents to be the time when they realize that other people besides themselves will be influencing their children and that their children are no longer babies.

Sending a child to school is often a highly emotional time for parents. They are acknowledging that their child is growing up and that they must let him go out into the world. Many parents also are wrapped up in memories and impressions of their own school experience.

Because parents are so emotionally involved in their own impressions of school, they may have expectations or fears that make it hard for them to relate to their child's school experience. Whether parents loved or hated school, they need to realize what impact school can have on a child, as well as how they can help their child deal with school responsibly and have the most enriching experience possible.

## How Do Schools Encourage Responsibility?

No teacher can magically bestow on a child a sense of responsibility. However, many of the expectations that good schools place on students, such as working with other students in a spirit of cooperation and team effort, competing with a sense of sportsmanship and fair play, getting to class on time, respecting teachers and school workers, respecting property, planning and completing assigned work independently, learning rules, and contributing to class discussions, encourage the development of responsibility. Over time, children internalize these expectations and learn the self-control and commitment that ultimately contribute to their acceptance of family and work responsibilities.

Schools also can nurture a sense of responsibility through open discussion of the issues that confront us all. For example, an elementary school science class may talk about pollution problems exacerbated by Styrofoam cups from fast-food restaurants. A high school science class may debate about the ethical problems that surround research testing on animals or the moral dilemmas suggested by recent discoveries in genetics. In social studies, second graders might talk about the importance of laws and rules and working together to solve community problems. Older students might discuss the civil rights movement, the history of race relations, and the importance of responsible government. In a health class, adolescents may be taught responsible sexual behavior by learning how to protect themselves from sexually transmitted diseases and by discussing what it means to respect oneself and the feelings of others. Some schools even offer specific classes in values.

## Why Some Schools Don't Make the Grade

For several years, and especially in recent months, Americans have been complaining that their schools have not been doing their job in meeting the needs of children. Parents and business leaders claim that students do not learn even basic skills, much less how to be productive and responsible members of society.

When schools were first established in this country, the study of values and moral development was an integral part of formal education. Puritan children learned how to read by using the Bible or *The Pilgrim's Progress*, a story in which characters confront many ethical dilemmas. In the latter part of the nineteenth century and into the twentieth century, children read stories about the values of hard work, kindness, honesty, and courage.

During the 1960s and 1970s, schools largely gave up playing the role of moral educators. No one was willing to state what values to teach, at the risk of inviting protests from groups who asked, "Why those values and not our values?" The schools, and therefore society at large, handed over the responsibility for a moral education to families alone. At the same time, the traditional family was also going through major restructuring. The divorce rate rose, families separated or joined with other families, the number of single parents increased, and more families were headed by two-career couples. Sadly the teaching of values fell to commercial television, which condoned violence, breaking the law, materialism, and casual sex. Clearly these were not the values most people would choose for their children to learn. By the late 1980s harried parents began looking back to the schools to provide guidance for their children.

Increasingly educators, parents, and politicians are seeing that the teaching of most subjects cannot be done in a vacuum, that values must be a part of the curriculum as they were in the past. There have been genuine attempts to improve the educational system in this country, from both an academic and a social point of view. In *The Good High School*, educator Sara Lawrence Lightfoot, Ph.D., cites a school in suburban Boston in which students and teachers work together on a "Fairness Committee" to make recommendations for dealing with disciplinary problems.

Private businesses are also becoming involved in the schools. To address their concern that the schools are not turning out an adequately trained work force, companies participating in the Boston Compact (an agreement between businesses and schools), for example, have guaranteed jobs and scholarships to any high school graduate. In return, the school system has pledged to improve test scores and attendance.

There also has been a resurgence in public support for making classes in morality and values a part of the school curriculum. In a special report, "Educating the Moral Child," in the November 1988 issue of *Principal*, Dr. Thomas Lickona writes that moral education is making a comeback: "Gallup Polls in recent years indicate that more than 80 percent of parents want public schools to teach moral values. Communities are discovering that despite pluralism, they can find common moral ground."

In the article, Dr. Lickona groups the list of values identified for a program in the Baltimore County Public Schools in Maryland under two universal values, which he calls "the fourth and fifth R's": respect and responsibility. He describes them as follows: "Respect tells us to value ourselves, other people, and the natural environment on which all life depends. Responsibility tells us to help our neighbor, to give back something to the persons and communities that gave to us, to alleviate suffering, and to do what we can to make a better world." He then provides two examples of schools (Birch Meadow Elementary School in

Reading, Massachusetts, and Winkelman Elementary School in Chicago) that implemented a values program to create a caring and just community of teachers and students. Both schools reported a greatly improved moral environment in which people were nicer to each other and everyone took more responsibility for the school.

## Education Begins at Home

By the time children enter school at around the age of five or six, they have already had several years of growing and learning. Their first and most important educators are their parents.

Parents can do a great number of things to help their children prepare for school. They can talk to their babies, sing to them, read to them, and provide them with opportunities to explore. Toddlers can be encouraged to find a special place for their books and can learn to value and take care of them.

Children are naturally curious and want to learn everything. Parents can encourage this sense of wonder and joy in discovery by helping them identify colors and sounds, count things, throw a ball, build with blocks, and draw with crayons. Parents can open up a new and fascinating world for their children by taking them on walks around the neighborhood, going to the bank or the store, visiting a library or a zoo, going to a swimming pool, or taking a ride on a bus or a train.

Parents also can prepare children for social responsibilities at school by teaching them to share, to ask for things they want, to use the toilet, to work and play by themselves, to pick up their things after they are finished with them, and to care about others' feelings. By the time they

**131**

enter school, children also need to feel comfortable about being away from parents for a few hours. If parents feel that their child does not yet have the skills or social maturity to go to kindergarten at the age of five, they might be wise to wait a year and to spend that time helping their child mature.

Many children spend years in day care or go to a preschool before they enter kindergarten. Naturally the transition from home to school is not as severe for these children. Parents who question whether or not preschool is necessary may find some help from educator David Elkind, Ph.D., in *Miseducation: Preschoolers at Risk.* He believes that being with children their same age and other adults can help children socially. "Because the range of toys and equipment is much greater than can be provided at home," he writes, "the nursery school offers additional opportunities for the child to enhance a sense of autonomy, initiative and healthy development." However, if parents are able to provide a variety of social and educational experiences, Dr. Elkind does not feel that preschool is essential.

Melitta J. Cutright, Ph.D., director of communications and programs for National PTA in Chicago, offers further advice in *The National PTA Talks to Parents: How to Get the Best Education for Your Child:* "For an only child, a child with few playmates in the neighborhood, a shy child or a child who lives in a small house or apartment, preschool is probably beneficial. Preschool allows children to learn to function without their parents, to relate to other caring adults, to deal with other children individually and in groups, to make friends, to play with different toys, to show and tell about things that are important to them." Preschool also has been shown to be valuable for children who come from lower-income families, non-English-speaking families, and for children with physical, mental, or emotional disabilities.

Most parents naturally want their children to have the

best start possible. But Dr. Elkind warns against hurrying a child to learn reading, math, and other academic subjects. He cautions that such pressures can result in emotional and learning problems, including early burnout. Instead, children need plenty of time to play and exercise their own creative abilities whether they are in preschool or at home.

Before the first day of school, parents can also help their child prepare by making sure he knows his full name, address, and telephone number. He should also be able to follow simple directions. A visit to the school and a rehearsal of what will happen will also reassure a child that going to school is an exciting experience to look forward to, rather than something to fear or be anxious about. Parents can also help by *not* expressing how they felt on their first day of school. Stories from parents about how nervous they were or how wonderful school was might set up false expectations in children and color their own impressions.

Even though a child is well prepared, parents should not be surprised by first-day nerves or a few days of uncertainty. Going to school is a big adjustment. The rules of behavior and the comfortable routines that have been established at home are likely to differ from those found in school. The structure of the day, the expected codes of conduct, the systems of reward and punishment all change markedly from home to school.

## Ongoing Support

Once a child has successfully entered school, the parents' role does not come to an end. Rather, it changes to support the new challenges he encounters. Parents also continue to be important guides in learning responsibility. Teachers influence children for only five or six hours a day in a group situation. Parents guide them the rest of the time.

In elementary school, children learn the basic skills that form the foundation for their future in school. Academically they learn to read, write, and add and subtract. Socially they learn how to listen to the teacher and other students, how to cooperate with a group, and how to work by themselves. They also are encouraged to move from a self-centered focus on their own goals to a consideration of the group's goals, which means supporting others' achievements and understanding others' failures.

By the time a child enters middle school or junior high school, he needs to be prepared for a new set of challenges and responsibilities. Along with a set of basic academic skills, here's what one principal expects of older children: "They should be able to move from one place in the building to another in a respectable manner by themselves. We expect them to make the transition from home to school and to keep up with their belongings. They should be able to organize themselves, demonstrate some independence and complete the tasks they begin. And they should be able to get along with each other, which can sometimes be harder than all of the rest of the pieces."

Parents can best help their child by taking an interest in his school experience. As discussed by Tom and Harriet Sobol in *Your Child in School,* such interest can take the form of expecting the child to do well and treating him as a capable person, and not labeling him or letting the school label him. Parents also should get into the habit of having regular conversations about school. Dinnertime is often a good occasion to ask the child about his day. However, a simple question such as "What did you learn in school today?" or "How was school today?" is likely to result in limited responses such as "Nothing" or "Fine." Parents can encourage talk about school by asking more specific questions about certain subjects, friends, after-school activities, or homework. These might include "What did your teacher say about your math homework?''; ''Did you read a story in class today? What was it about?''; ''What games did you play outside during recess?''; ''What pictures did you draw?'' or ''What songs did you sing?''

If the child seems reluctant to talk, parents might consider starting a conversation by sharing something of their own activities. For example, a parent may say, ''I'm learning a new computer system at work. It's complicated, but interesting, and I'm sure I'll master it eventually,'' ''Mary and I finally managed to solve a problem we'd been working on for a long time. We found the information we needed in one of the manuals, then figured out a plan, and tried it,'' or ''We celebrated John's birthday today by buying him lunch.'' Parents can then move into asking the child about his day.

Parents' involvement in school sometimes can take the form of limiting involvement and respecting their child's right to make his own decisions and to learn from the consequences. Particularly as a child gets older and is faced with more choices about course work and extracurricular activities, parents can be helpful by talking about his options and perhaps making suggestions, rather than forcing their own agenda. Insisting that a child study a musical instrument or try out for a varsity sport is much more likely to cement dislikes than to foster great enthusiasm. However, parents should encourage their child to try a number of activities to find out what he really enjoys and what he is best at.

Perhaps the most difficult disassociation for parents to make is in trying to view a child's achievements or difficulties in school as separate from their abilities as parents. It is hard for parents not to feel responsible for everything their child does. In fact, it is the *child's* job to pay attention in the classroom, to get along with his peers, to do his homework, and to adjust to the preferences of a new teacher. Parents can't do any of these things for him and will only frustrate and anger themselves and their child if they try. They can, however, let their child know that they are available to provide help and support when he needs it, without nagging or interfering with his peer relationships or his interaction with the teacher. A child has to learn how to smooth out life's rough edges for himself. "Parents always want their children to be the best and the smartest; that's natural," said the mother of three school-age youngsters. "But we need to pull back from that attitude and give them space to make their own mistakes. Otherwise they won't learn for themselves."

No matter how well a child seems to be doing with schoolwork, he still needs his parents to continue to be teachers and advisors throughout his academic career. Even the best schools do not always offer as enriched a curriculum or as much personal attention as children need. Acquiring new skills at school should not result in a loss of closeness with parents. Reading aloud to a school-age child, even after he learns how to read for himself, for example, teaches him that learning to read will not cost him his parents' attention. Going to a museum, taking nature walks, showing him how to use the library, teaching him to cook, playing games, and playing musical instruments together are all ways to share family time while augmenting the lessons learned at school and strengthening the child's family ties.

Parents may also remind themselves to be patient and not to get discouraged if their child progresses slowly at school. "People tend to do what they feel good about doing," the Sobols write. "Help your child feel good about his ability to use his mind!" The balance between limiting critical pressure and making sure a child is doing his best in school is sometimes difficult to achieve. Frequent checks on a child's progress by both parents and teachers can help them identify early on where he is struggling and needs help and whether or not a little push is sufficient.

## Who's Responsible for Homework

Homework assignments provide an important opportunity for a child to assume new responsibilities, to develop self-discipline, and to cultivate good work habits. It helps him practice reading, learn to make decisions, and exercise judgment, and reinforces what was learned in class. However, it can also become an unpleasant battleground between parents and child.

Lecturing or punishing a child who is neglecting his homework can be counterproductive. Nagging generally increases tension at home. Ignoring the issue invites criticism from the teacher, which can lower a child's self-esteem. Threats can result in a fierce argument. What, then, are parents to do?

Parents need to remember that children do not have an innate ability to complete homework carefully, accurately, and on time. The necessary discipline and organizational skills are acquired only with practice. Parents can help cultivate productive habits by showing an interest in homework assignments, offering help with problem subjects if necessary, and providing one-on-one attention that teachers can't give. Parents also need to communicate the fact that they consider homework an important responsibility. Parents also are advised not to invest their own egos in their child's performance and to remember that a child needs to be allowed to make his own mistakes. This is not to say that a child should be left to flounder. There *are* practical ways to help a child avoid becoming overwhelmed by homework:

• **Decide how much help to give a child with his home-**

**work.** Teachers often differ in their expectations and philosophy. One asks parents to take a hands-off approach, saying, "Let your child take all the responsibility for his work because I want to see what he can produce without your help." But another believes strongly in parental involvement and says, "I appreciate your sitting down with your child when his homework is complete and reviewing it with him." If parents disagree sharply with a teacher's attitudes, they may wish to discuss their differences in a parent-teacher conference or a telephone call. As long as parents and teachers distinguish between helping a child develop good work habits and doing his work for him, a compromise is usually possible.

- **Offer help and show a child how to get help himself.** If a child doesn't know the meaning of a word, parents can encourage him to look it up in a dictionary. Once in a while, it's okay to give him the meaning so that he can get on with his work. (After all, when he was a preschooler, his parents gladly supplied the answers to his questions. A child shouldn't feel that, once he's in school, every new learning experience includes frustration.) If a child has trouble with an assignment, a parent could work out an example with him. When parents review his homework, they might say something such as, "I see a mistake; maybe you want to check it over again" or "Is that the neatest you can be?" Then they can step back and let him decide whether he wants to redo the assignment. If he chooses not to he'll have to take the consequences in the classroom. (Parents need to keep in mind that their standards and the teacher's standards may be quite different. What parents find appalling may suit the teacher just fine and vice versa.) When an assignment is completed in a manner that parents approve of, they can make a point of praising their child for a job well done.

Parents also can help a child organize homework and suggest different ways of studying a subject so that assigned tasks can be completed more efficiently. Suggestions might include making sure a child has all the materials necessary, such as paper, pencils, and books; using strategies for finding important ideas in a text and for taking brief notes to help him remember; deciding how much time different tasks might take; listing what needs to be done; and prioritizing assignments.

- **Agree on when the homework should be completed.** Although a child needs to be responsible for his homework, parents can establish a framework for getting it done by deciding with a child when homework should be undertaken. Some children really need to blow off steam when they get out of school, so a two-hour break might be allowed. Others will procrastinate indefinitely and need a strict rule that says: No playing until all your homework is completed. Many families bar television watching until school assignments are finished. Whatever the schedule that works best for a child, it should be followed consistently. Parents can then check to make sure the homework is complete and that it is placed in a book bag or notebook to take to school the next day. If parents find that homework hasn't been completed, they also need to be consistent with previously agreed-upon consequences. This might include arranging extra time to do the homework or limiting of privileges until a child catches up with assignments.

- **Try not to let a child's homework dominate a parent's life.** If a child needs or wants help, parents can establish a mutually acceptable way to provide it. Parents may set up a consistent time after dinner to answer homework questions in order to avoid such situations as being bombarded with requests upon arriving home tired after a long day at the office. One mother has found this solution to the problem: "I let my child choose when she will do her homework, but I've told her that I'm available to provide help only if she does it at a time that is convenient for me. If she chooses to wait until late in the evening when I'm tired, then she knows she is on her own." Other parents are content to be more flexible and make themselves available for help with homework whenever they are needed. The important thing is for parents to determine ahead of time the means by which they are available.

- **Provide a comfortable setting in which to work.** Ideally a child will have his own desk for doing schoolwork, but a corner of the dining room table will do as long as it is available to him whenever he is ready to settle down. Children need enough space to spread out their papers and books and sufficient light to see what they are doing. Don't assume the workplace has to be located in some remote corner of the house. While homework usually cannot be done well in front of the television, not everyone needs absolute silence in which to concentrate. If a child prefers to be located close to the household hustle and bustle rather than isolated from the action and proves that he can do his work there (even with the radio blaring or the television on), it is safe to be guided by his preferences.

- **Try not to allow other family problems to interfere with homework.** Sometimes a child adopts a defiant attitude toward schoolwork as a way to punish Mom and Dad for unrelated wrongs. A child whose parents are in the throes of divorce, pressured by the demands of two careers, or worried about other children or their own elderly parents is subject to severe stresses that often manifest themselves in unexpected ways. A child may claim he is unable to concentrate, exhibit constant restlessness, become depressed, lose interest in schoolwork, express anger and give up because he feels no one cares, or seek ways to be out of the house as much as possible. It is important to deal with the real sources of distress so that academic problems are not added on top of other emotional upheavals. Letting him know that his schoolwork (as well as other aspects of his life) remains important gives a child an anchor during rough times.

- **Support the concept of homework, even if the assignments seem less than appropriate.** Homework may at times consist of completing a dozen or so mimeographed drills and practice lessons, for example. Parents may be right to conclude that this assignment seems to be busywork that benefits no one. If a child balks at doing such time-consuming, boring work, parents can help him learn something the teacher probably had not intended, which is that life is often full of mundane work and that not every action is productive or challenging. Parents should let their child know, however, that while he cannot see the point of doing such work, it is still his responsibility to do it. When there is a pattern of repetitive, non-thought-provoking work, parents may want to discuss the issue with the teacher in private.

## The Issue of Report Cards

For both parents and children, report card time can be a reason for pride or a reason for high anxiety. A report card provides tangible evidence of how a child is doing in school both academically and behaviorally. A good report card might bring sighs of relief, while a bad report card can result in angry arguments between parents and children.

If parents have frequently checked how a child is doing on homework and have had contact with the teacher through conferences or phone calls, they shouldn't be surprised by what they see on the report card. As Dr. Melitta J.

Cutright writes, parents should remind themselves that "report cards are a measure of how students are doing in school, not of students' worth as individuals or of parents' success as parents. Also, report cards measure what has happened in the past; they show what is over and can't be changed. For this reason, if report cards are not good, they should be used as a platform for change, rather than as a reason for punishment."

Telling a child that he is lazy or stupid or revoking privileges because of a bad report card is unlikely to be effective. In fact it might even make the situation worse. Instead parents can try to discuss a report card calmly with their child and work out a mutually agreed-upon plan for making improvements. First, however, parents need to praise a child for any strengths and accomplishments shown on the card. Then they can talk about why there are problems. A drop in a single grade may be a sign that a child does not understand new concepts or material. A comparison with past report cards, along with a review of teacher comments on homework and grades on tests, may show that a low grade is part of a consistent pattern. Parents may also find by looking at past report cards that there has actually been improvement in some areas.

Ways to improve grades then can be discussed. A child may not be allowing enough time to complete homework or to study for a test. He may not have adequate materials or a good place to study with adequate light, space, and freedom from distractions. He may need some help with study habits, such as how to read for information, how to take notes, and how to organize materials. He may need some help in understanding a concept, in which case a parent might be able to go over the material with him step-by-step. If parents themselves do not understand a subject, they can admit it and then help their child by finding a tutor who can assist him. If the parents and child cannot determine what the problem is, a call to the teacher may be needed.

Some report cards indicate behavioral rather than academic problems. In talking with their child, parents might be able to find out why he has trouble concentrating in school or why he disrupts the class. He might be bored with the material, not understand what is being taught, or have a visual or hearing problem that is interfering with learning, an emotional problem related to upsets at home or disagreements with the teacher, or a learning disability.

Parents probably will need to meet with the teacher to discuss further any learning or behavioral problems and what can be done to help their child. Many children can benefit by learning in a different way, such as using a typewriter or a computer instead of writing by hand, reading from comic books instead of texts, or building with blocks rather than just by seeing numbers on paper. Children also can have their eyes or ears tested or be tested for disabilities such as dyslexia (a reading problem). Some children will benefit from counseling to help them with an emotional problem.

## Parents and Teachers as Partners

Before a child goes to school, he has had the benefit of growing and learning under the guidance and teaching of his parents. When he enters preschool, kindergarten, or grade school, his teacher becomes another major influence in his life. By treating students with respect, sparking their curiosity, and following through on promises, a teacher is a key model of responsible behavior.

In his impassioned book *On Being a Teacher*, educator Jonathan Kozol explains in part the importance and art of teaching:

> *Teaching and learning are inseparable. The teacher is in the classroom to make learning possible; his act is principally, then, an* enabling *act. . . . This means removing the student's fears of authority, his fears of being ridiculed, his fears of the subject, his fears of failing. It means granting him the dignified status of student—someone capable of mastering the subject. It means allowing him that which goes with dignity, the right to express his views and advance his interests, the right to ask questions, the right to disagree, the right even not to understand. It means assuming that although he may be in the course only to pass it or get a high grade he is able to get much more than that from it.*

Most parents are aware that teachers are also human. Even the best of teachers are often hindered by the huge task of trying to teach many students of different backgrounds and abilities a variety of subjects with limited time and materials. Time is also taken up by record keeping, discipline, and special events. So how do parents know whether their child has a good teacher?

Clues to a good teacher will come through parent-teacher conferences, the amount and kind of homework assigned to children, and the child's own reactions to school. Some schools allow parents to visit and observe a class on occasion. Parents might also think back to what they liked about teachers who inspired them. Other questions parents might want to consider in evaluating a teacher are these, adapted from Dr. Cutright:

- Does the teacher know each child's needs, interests, and special talents, and understand the way each child learns best?
- Does the teacher talk with parents at the beginning of the school year, then maintain contact with open communication about any academic or behavioral problems?
- Does regularly assigned homework enrich what is taught in class? Does the teacher provide parents with suggestions on how to help children with homework?
- Does the teacher expect all children to learn and help them to do so?
- Is the teacher caring, friendly, and enthusiastic?
- Does the teacher praise children and avoid ridicule, thereby building their self-esteem?
- Are clear and fair class rules established early in the year and then consistently enforced?
- Does the teacher treat children fairly without playing favorites?
- Are teaching methods varied and is learning presented as fun through such things as games, music, role-playing, bulletin board displays, and group projects?
- Does the teacher welcome parent participation by suggesting how parents can help children at home?

Identifying an incompetent teacher might be more difficult. A child's complaints that a teacher ridicules or picks on him need to be taken seriously. Parents first can identify whether an incident is isolated or whether a problem is continuous. Then they can recall what their child's relationships with teachers have been in the past in order to check whether there is a pattern of problems. If the trouble seems to be with only one teacher, parents should arrange a conference to hear the other side of the story. By being open but not accusatory about their child's upset, parents may be able to clear up any misunderstandings and work with the teacher on ways to improve the situation.

If, after talking with a teacher, parents believe he is incompetent, they may consider talking with the principal. However, this action runs the risk of preventing any good relationship between the parents and the teacher. They may be able to solve the problem with the principal, or perhaps get their child transferred to another class. Beyond this, there may be little they can do. Removing a poor teacher from a teaching staff is extremely difficult and often a long process. Parents may instead consider getting extra help for their child in a subject, such as a tutor or a summer class, or helping their child get through the rest of the school year with as little conflict as possible.

The best way to help make home and school (the two major influences in a child's life) compatible is for parents and teachers to work together in a productive partnership based on mutual respect.

## Parent-Teacher Conferences

Many parents view a talk with their child's teacher with apprehension. This tension can be reduced if parents trust that both they and their child's teacher have the best interests of the child in mind. Remember that many teachers are also parents who understand what it's like to be on the other side of the desk. To get the most out of conferences with the teacher, parents can think ahead about the topics for discussion. Based on their own observations and comments from their child about school, they also can come prepared to pose specific questions, to express their concerns, and to solicit concrete advice.

Parents need to be prepared to listen without overreacting to the teacher's criticisms or engaging in a spirited defense. It's not easy for parents to hear a negative report on their child. It often feels like an implied criticism of the parents themselves. But defensiveness often leads to parents and teachers blaming each other without finding a solution. Parents should try to remember that the teacher sees their child in a very different environment. His professional insights are worthy of consideration and respect and are most often helpful. Teachers also welcome any information and impressions parents can share that will help them better understand a student.

It's important, too, for parents not to criticize the teacher's technique. They can diffuse a potentially tense situation by expressing their opinions tactfully ("I think Hallie would have an easier time in science class if she had some studying to do at home") or by stating a fact ("Sometimes Brian feels left out of the classroom discussions"). Making judgments or dispensing advice may only invite hostility.

The annual conference may also be more relaxed if parents have had several informal contacts with the teacher beforehand. Teachers often make a point of meeting parents at the beginning of the school year, then keeping in regular contact. Jonathan Kozol writes about the need for parents and teachers to create "a sense of common cause" and urges teachers to visit parents at home so that they can socialize informally. In communities where this is impractical, Parent Teacher Association (PTA) meetings are another popular place for building a good relationship. It is also reasonable to ask that a teacher stay in touch not only when there are problems to report but when the child has achieved something positive as well. A message from a teacher should not always elicit the thought, "John must be in trouble," but rather, at least on some occasions, "I wonder if John has won another award."

Some schools encourage children to attend a conference with their parents and teachers. Whether or not this is the case, parents need to make a point of talking about the conference with their child. They can mention any statements the teacher made about his strengths as well as his weaknesses. Comments should be factual rather than judgmental; a statement such as, "Mrs. Delgado says that you aren't very comfortable with doing multiplication tables," is much easier for a child to accept than such comments as, "You just aren't paying enough attention in math class." Parents can then work with their child to plan ways to make improvements.

Beside fostering a strong partnership with teachers, parents can help improve the overall quality of their child's education by becoming more involved with the schools. Children generally get the best possible education and learn the most about being a good student and a good citizen in school systems where parental input is actively encouraged and respected. Participating in the PTA, attending school board meetings, keeping in touch with other parents in the community, volunteering to assist in a classroom or the school library, and chaperoning field trips are all effective ways parents can be a part of their child's education. "The first thing I became involved in was the PTA," said one mother who recently moved to a new community. "That's where you get your information, that's where the school and the parents work together, and that's where you build real communication."

## The Working Parent's Dilemma

Because so many children grow up either in single-parent families or in families where both parents work, attending events at school and arranging parent-teacher conferences can be a big problem. Volunteer chaperones for class trips and student dances are hard for schools to find. "My son's teacher thinks I'm not interested in his progress," says one working mother. "But when I don't work, I don't get paid, and our family just can't afford to be without my income." A study conducted by Susan Kontos of Purdue University found, ironically, that parents who need the greatest support, such as single and divorced mothers, are often held in the lowest esteem by teachers.

Teachers, for their part, often resist being asked to stay late in school or to give up evenings that already are filled with grading papers and creating lesson plans and caring for their own families, in order to accommodate working parents.

Fortunately there are some solutions that do not impose greatly on either parent or teacher. Even if parents are not able to attend every open house or most parent-teacher conferences, they should make an effort to meet the teacher at the beginning of the school year. At that time parents shouldn't hesitate to explain the limitations on their time and encourage the teacher to telephone if he needs to. Communicating through notes or letters is another relatively easy way to stay in touch. Divorced parents may also be able to work out a system between themselves of alternating attendance at conferences. And some teachers, who arrive at school at an early hour anyway, may be willing to arrange a conference before school begins and a parent has to be at work.

## At Home Alone after School

Many working parents also face the problem of what to do with children who arrive home from school two to three hours before they themselves can get home from work.

These kids are known as *latchkey children*. Estimates vary of from two to 13 million children who spend time alone at home after school every day.

Opinions differ as to whether or not school children and teens should be allowed to stay home alone. Studies have shown that some children may feel lonely and fearful. One third-grade student confessed to researchers that she often hid in a closet until her parents returned home from work. Other children may become bored and be tempted to get into trouble as serious as experimenting with drugs and alcohol.

Experts do agree that children younger than 10 should probably not be left alone. Of course this depends on the maturity of a child and how he feels about it. Before deciding to leave a child alone, however, parents need to make every effort to explore as many options for child care as they can. This might include arranging to have a child go to a neighbor's house, attend a day-care facility that has an after-school program, stay with a baby-sitter, or take part in programs that are available in such community places as the YMCA, the YWCA, the local library, or at the school itself.

When economic or logistical reasons make it necessary to leave a child alone for periods of time, there are some ways to help him deal with the experience:

- **Parents should communicate safety precautions with the idea of instilling caution rather than creating fear.** While a child must know how to reach a parent, a neighbor, the police, or the fire department in the event of an emergency, blunt warnings, such as ''Don't open the door to anyone'' or ''Don't let anyone know you are home alone,'' are more likely to increase anxiety than to keep a child safe. Instead, the child can be told that he will likely feel more confident about being home if he knows exactly what to do. Then parents can make sure that he is prepared with instructions on what to do in any situation, including how to carry a house key out of sight; what to do if he misses a bus or ride home; what to do if there is bad weather; how to report a fire, call the police, or react to a medical emergency; and what to do if a stranger follows him home or knocks at the door.

- **Parents need to recognize that allowing a child to care for himself is an important statement about his maturity.** Sometimes latchkey children receive mixed messages from their parents. "During the initial stages of self-care the child is torn between feelings of anxiety and independence," write psychologist Lynette Long, Ph.D., and educator Thomas Long, Ed.D., in *The Handbook for Latchkey Children and Their Parents.* "The parent needs to recognize both these feelings and provide the child with more understanding and freedom when coming home from work. Failure to do so will only make the child's adjustment more difficult by causing frustration because he is expected to act like an adult part of the day and a child as soon as his parents walk through the door."

- **Parents also should maintain good communication.** They can have their child call a neighbor or a relative as soon as he arrives home. He also should know how to and be encouraged to get in touch with parents at work. Parents can also try to call whenever possible, and leave little love notes for a child to find when he arrives home. When parents arrive home, they should make an effort to spend a few minutes with their child and reassure him of their love and attention.

- **Parents should not overload a child with too much responsibility.** Many parents feel they have to fill up a child's time alone and so heap on him too many household chores or other structured activities. "I don't mind being alone, but sometimes my mother gives me so many things to do that I feel as though I'm the parent and she's the child,'' complained one 10-year-old who tends her six-year-old brother for two hours every day after school. However, parents can help their child plan his time alone so that he doesn't become bored or just watch television.

- **With the input of the child, parents should establish rules for being home alone.** These may include not turning on the television until homework is done, not inviting friends over without advance approval, being able to fix a snack but not using the stove, and not letting anyone into the house.
- **Parents should try to come home when they say they will or make sure they call to say they'll be late.** Dependability is crucial to a child's sense of security.

## After-School Activities

Within reason, after-school activities can enrich the lives of young children, but it is important to guard against over-scheduling. Children may become simply exhausted and unable to use their energy productively for anything as important as unstructured play. When the week begins to look like this: Monday, violin lessons; Tuesday, swimming lessons; Wednesday, Spanish class; and Thursday, computer class, it's time to rethink the amount of structure that is being imposed on a child's life.

By the middle-school or junior-high years students often seek out extracurricular activities on their own. Whether it is the student newspaper, student council, a language club, music lessons, or a sports team, many schools offer an array of activities diverse enough to appeal to almost everyone. Older children should be encouraged to choose their own extracurricular activities as much as possible, as long as these don't interfere with their academic responsibilities or make them too tired. This guideline applies to after-school jobs as well.

A child should not be pressured to join a special club or to pursue a particular hobby. The mother who never made the cheerleading squad or the father who always wanted to be a painter rather than an engineer may pressure a child into following the road they failed to take, an approach that can fuel conflict and destroy the pleasure of any activity.

Although extracurricular activities can be challenging and educational, they should not become a source of stress in a child's life. Schoolwork and family life constitute a child's main responsibilities; extracurricular activities should be pursued mostly for fun.

## Fear or Dislike of School

Not every child flourishes in school. Many go through phases of particular unhappiness. "I'm bored" is a cry that just about every parent hears at one time or another. Other children may complain of frequent stomachaches or headaches in an effort to stay home from school.

If complaints are relatively mild and a child's grades do not change markedly, there's not too much cause for concern. A child may be going through a rough period socially or not hitting it off too well with a particular teacher. Gentle questions usually can uncover the source of the discontent. Without being impatient or unsympathetic, parents can consider that there's nothing wrong with reminding a child that school, like other elements of life, has its ups and downs and that sometimes people have to fulfill their responsibilities even when they are not too happy about them.

On the other hand, if there are physical manifestations of distress, such as stomachaches; changes in eating or sleeping patterns; or a regression to childish behavior, such as bedwetting or crying, the problem requires attention. Parents need to avoid criticizing a child for his fears. After trying to find out from their child what the problem is, parents should talk with the teacher. School counselors and administrators, too, may be able to provide some guidance about the severity of the problem, possible causes, and where to go for help.

The school years are a major part of everyone's life. Through the help and support of teachers and parents, school can be a rewarding and enjoyable experience and a strong foundation for learning how to act responsibly when meeting the challenges of the adult world.

• • • • • • • • • • • • • • • • • • • • • • • • • • • • • •

## Parents ask:

*By the time Steven was 17, he was probably the laziest kid on earth—except when it came to his lifelong passion for airplanes. In his senior year it seemed unlikely he would graduate from high school. Against my better judgment I finally stepped in and basically did all his homework just to get him through the year. He did graduate, but just barely. Three years later he began to grow up. Now he's got a great job as a pilot, he takes care of business, and I'm really proud of him. I know that what I did went against all the rules in all the books, but I'm glad I let him off the hook when I did. If he hadn't graduated, his life might have been ruined. Now my 14-year-old seems to be headed in the same general direction. He has little interest in anything else but his art. On principle I hesitate to step in to "save" him, too. But I wonder. Is propping up a kid until he's ready to grow up really such a bad thing?*

When a child has an interest in life that excludes all other schoolwork responsibilities, there is nothing wrong with a parent helping him over the tough spots and allowing him to grow into what he loves most. Doing so may bring a parent and child closer. However, if a child has extremely limited interests, it's possible that bailing him out will only cover a possible learning problem or some difficulty with authority and the demands of the outside world. Moreover, if a parent and child find themselves in terrible struggles over schoolwork, it's time to get outside help, such as a tutor or a study partner. Helping becomes a big problem when a child's school performance comes

**155**

to mean more to a parent than to a child. Then the situation has gone too far. Otherwise, this parent should relax and help her child where necessary. Maybe together they can learn something.

# Part III

......

# What's Next?

"I'M NOT SURE HOW A PERSON FINDS A PLACE IN THE WORLD, SON, BUT I HAVE A SUGGESTION."

# CHAPTER SIX

• • • • • •

# Your Child's Place in a Changing World

As children near adolescence and begin to participate more independently in the life of their community, they have more opportunities to practice what they have learned about being responsible. They also find their fledgling sense of responsibility being tested in new ways.

No matter how well they have been raised or how high their levels of confidence are, preteens and teenagers are faced with some hard choices. What will a 12-year-old do if her peers urge her to drink alcohol at a party or to smoke a cigarette? Will she join a crowd that taunts someone who is disabled, speaks with a foreign accent, or is a member of a different ethnic or racial group? Or will she empathize with and defend that person? What will a teenager do if she meets an older boy who wants to be sexually intimate?

A child's actions in such situations directly impact her health and well-being, and a positive, responsible response reflects her belief in herself. However, behaving responsibly involves far more than just staying out of trouble. It also involves making positive choices. What will a child do to improve the society in which she lives? Will she look for constructive ways to help those who are less fortunate? Does she have leadership potential? Will she choose to honor her obligations to her work and family life as well? Parents cannot provide all the answers. Ultimately, children become the adults *they* want to be.

Parents who begin early to teach responsible behavior are

likely to see the benefits of their work during their child's teenage years. However, their work is not completed when a child becomes a teenager. In many ways, parental guidance is even more important in helping a teenager not to lose sight of her values and sense of responsibility while dealing with the daily realities of a sometimes harsh life. Parents can provide encouragement to teens to assert their autonomy with increasing vigor, to make more of their own judgments, and to demonstrate a more mature knowledge of right and wrong.

What makes some young people able to make constructive choices, while others take self-destructive paths?

In large part, the difference lies between those who are hopeful and those who feel hopeless. A high self-esteem helps a child face life's opportunities and risks. A child who believes in her own potential and worth and who looks forward to the future stands the best chance of maneuvering past danger and temptation. In the face of peer pressure she can say, "I don't need to compromise my safety to prove myself. I have value on my own terms." Because she has a strong sense of herself, she is psychologically equipped to care about herself, her family, and other people, and is ready to make a meaningful contribution to the world around her. She is assertive, not passive; she tells herself, "The choices I make have an effect on my own life and on the lives of other people. I *can* make a difference."

By contrast, an alienated child thinks, "I have no value to myself or others." Without a strong sense of personal worth, such a child is vulnerable to negative influences, including the lure of drugs and the enticement of careless sex. And because she doesn't feel good about herself or see a positive future ahead, it's hard for her to believe she could make a contribution to anything.

Teenagers in general struggle with a volatile mixture of debilitating feelings of insecurity and powerful feelings of immortality and invulnerability. As a result, they often define themselves in relation to their peers and are tempted to indulge in risky behavior without worrying about the consequences. They are both self-absorbed and interested in the world. They are capable of becoming passionately involved in the justice and fairness of political and social issues but often see these issues in only black-and-white terms. Their feelings of uncertainty about themselves often make it difficult for them to accept that there are generally shades of gray between both sides of a controversy.

Parents themselves once went through this process when they were teenagers. However, today many parents believe the world their teenagers face is more complicated and confusing than the one in which they came of age. Parents may feel the need for guidance in tackling sensitive issues, especially the problems of drugs, drinking, and teenage sex. They may also be looking for productive alternatives to self-destructive behavior to offer their teenagers.

Each generation also has had to deal with its own problems and issues, including war, economic depression, and racial unrest. However, as the world has increasingly become more of a global community with far-away problems getting closer to home, the worries adults have about teenagers have taken on an urgency unknown in simpler times. One study, quoted in a recent *Parents* magazine, shows some contrast between what teachers cited as important behavioral issues students in public school faced in the 1940s vs. what students were dealing with in the 1980s:

| 1940s | 1980s |
| --- | --- |
| 1. Talking | 1. Drug abuse |
| 2. Chewing gum | 2. Alcohol abuse |
| 3. Making noise | 3. Pregnancy |
| 4. Running in the halls | 4. Suicide |

| 1940s contd. | 1980s contd. |
|---|---|
| 5. Getting out of turn in line | 5. Rape |
| 6. Wearing improper clothing | 6. Robbery |
| 7. Not putting paper in waste-<br>baskets | 7. Assault |

While the issues on the second list have been human concerns for many people throughout history, they seem especially prominent now because they visibly seem to threaten young people in places previously thought to be safe. Incidents of violence against teachers and students have increased, and even grade-school children are offered drugs or alcohol by their classmates.

Current statistics might give parents added reason to fear for their children:

- Some 16,000 teenagers are killed every year in automobile accidents, most of which are a result of the use of alcohol or drugs.
- According to a recent survey of 16,000 students conducted by researchers at the University of Michigan, 85.7 percent of high school seniors had used alcohol in 1988, two-thirds of them within 30 days of the survey. The same study found that although the 57 percent figure of high school seniors who had used marijuana represented a lower figure from previous years, one-third of the students had tried other illicit and dangerous drugs, such as crack, LSD, or PCP. In the November 1988 issue of *Principal*, developmental psychologist Dr. Thomas Lickona reported that ''American youth show the highest level of drug abuse of any young people in the industrialized world.'' Dr. Lickona also reported that ''juvenile crime has steadily in-

creased. . . . [T]he rate of increase is greatest among the youngest age groups.''

- A study in Los Angeles, cited at an American Academy of Pediatrics conference in July 1989, showed that 31 percent of adolescents had their first sexual experience by age 14; 43 percent had sex between the ages of 15 and 18. In the last 20 years, teenage pregnancies have doubled; 80 percent of them are unintentional. Fewer than 10 percent of teenage girls who become unmarried mothers ever finish high school.

It's small wonder that parenting seems to be getting harder and more confusing. ''I'm really frightened about all the dangers Martin will be exposed to over the next few years,'' said one father. ''Sometimes I wish I could just lock him up until he is 21 and comes to his senses.''

Obviously that's not a practical approach. It is more realistic, even though difficult, to realize that most adolescents will eventually be tempted to experiment with sex, alcohol, or drugs. These things are intriguing to children, at least in part because they are designated off-limits. This does not mean that every child will try hard drugs, nor that she will continue using them. Not every teenager will inevitably have intercourse in her early teen years. After all, even though 43 percent are having sex between the ages of 15 and 18, 57 percent are not.

Being alert to and trying to prevent possible dangers does not mean overreacting to rebellious conduct or imposing sudden and harsh new restrictions on children. Realistically parents cannot completely control what their teenage child chooses to do. However, parents can and do have a right to express their opinions and their concerns, which are most effective when accompanied by accurate information on the consequences of dangerous behavior. And they can work with their children to establish and enforce fair rules.

When sensitive issues, such as substance abuse or sex, are raised, all of the strengths and weaknesses of the parent-child relationship come into sharp focus. While parents need to provide firm guidelines, they also need to allow a child the room to make her own decisions and to learn from her mistakes as long as no serious or lasting harm is being done. When kept within reasonable boundaries, a child's challenges to authority can be viewed as healthy expressions of greater independence.

Parents can let their child know they support her, as well as express how they feel about irresponsible behavior, without giving the impression they are trying to live her life for her. One approach might be to say, "I want the best things in life for you. And I know you probably feel pressure to do some things before you are ready or because you think it will make the other kids like you better. I can't force you to do what I want, but I think you should know how I feel and why I feel this way."

In *Between Parent and Teenager* Dr. Haim G. Ginott wrote, "Our response must differentiate between tolerance and sanction, between acceptance and approval. We tolerate much, but sanction little. A physician does not reject a patient because he bleeds. Though unpleasant, such behavior is tolerated; it is neither encouraged nor welcomed. It is merely accepted. Similarly, a parent can tolerate unlikable behavior without sanctioning it." Many parents may have difficulty understanding how they might express disapproval while not actually prohibiting something. One example might be willingly to pick up a daughter who has called home to say that she's had too much to drink and doesn't want to drive. In such a situation, a parent is caught between pride for the responsible behavior of calling and anger for the irresponsible behavior of drinking. The parent can tell her child she disapproves of drinking and that she is happy the child chose to call rather than risk her own and others' lives by trying to drive home.

Harsh threats tend to backfire. "Don't ever let me catch you drinking or you'll be grounded for six months!" is a sure way to provoke hostility, and it will greatly reduce the likelihood that a parent will be called on for help when a child most needs it.

## The Influences of the Media

The media, including newspapers, magazines, and especially television, have a powerful impact on a child's view of the world. Many of their influences are positive ones. For example, television exposes young people to a range of lifestyles and situations outside their immediate experience. Children growing up in rural areas may see their first portraits of urban life, and children who live in cities may get a glimpse of life in small towns. Preschoolers can learn their ABCs through educational programming, while older children can learn about life in other countries and cultures. They also can see some of their favorite stories come alive in television movies. Through stories, good television programs can model responsible behavior by illustrating the values of sharing and cooperation and by presenting sympathetic, generous, and responsible characters as heroes.

Television, of course, can also be a negative influence; kids are exposed to a great deal of information, and often misinformation, about sex, drugs, and alcohol. Some shows suggest that a world of drugs is glamorous. Drinking is nearly always shown in fun situations. Television couples engage in casual sex with no thought of the consequences. According to a 1988 Harris poll, American children hear an average of more than 14,000 sexual references and innuendos on television each year; fewer than 150 of these refer to birth control.

Television also portrays a world colored by violence and can convey the message that crime is a way to get what you want. Research shows that 12-year-old children who are regular television watchers have seen nearly 100,000 violent events, including 13,000 people violently destroyed. This savage behavior has been shown to desensitize children to the realities of violence in real life.

Other negative values implied by television, according to Dr. Thomas Lickona in *Raising Good Children*, include the ideas that sarcastic put-downs are funny, adults are stupid, women are inferior, the world is a terrible place because the focus is always on bad news, life is entertainment at the expense of creativity and hard work, and possessions make people happy.

Many racial, ethnic, religious, and handicapped groups are too often portrayed negatively and stereotypically. Teenagers themselves sometimes complain that the media present a distorted image of their lives. Partying, cutting school, making trouble, and showing a lack of concern for other people or their property is not the whole of their activities, say today's teens, but too often it is only these dramatic stories that make the nightly news or that provide good sitcom story lines.

Advertising on television and in magazines and newspapers can also have a negative influence. Although cigarette ads have been banned from television, they are still featured heavily in magazines and newspapers and on billboards. Tempting beer and wine ads are everywhere, especially in places where young people congregate, such as music concerts, sporting events, and recreational areas. When trendy new products are heavily promoted, as they often are during children's television programs, a child may feel pressured to acquire new possessions to keep pace with her peers.

Obviously it is neither practical nor desirable for parents to isolate their child from the press or to ban television from their home. The challenge for parents is to monitor their use and to encourage the child to be thoughtful about what she is reading or watching. Parents might watch television part of the time with her and comment on the behavior of characters in a program. For example, if a show portrays a drunken character as being funny or attractive, parents might say, "I don't think that guy is so charming after having a few drinks. I think it's sad." Asking a young child questions about the characters can also encourage conversation about values. A teenager, however, may resist the underlying purpose of teaching that is implied by such questions.

Parents also can bring attention to the media as positive sources of information. If parents see something in a newspaper or magazine about young people or that might be of interest to young people, they can ask their teenager's opinion when they have a chance. For example, "I saw an article in the newspaper that said American students don't know much about geography. Why do you think it's important to know where other countries are located?" or "I read a review about that movie that all the kids seem to like so much. The reviewer thought it was silly. What did you think of it?" Questions about current issues could also stimulate debate. A lively family discussion ensued when one mother said, "I read that our country will soon run out of landfill space. What do you think we're going to do with all our garbage when that happens?"

Newspapers, magazines, and television are all potentially useful tools in teaching values and responsibility if parents pay attention to them and help their child read or watch them intelligently. Parents can also encourage the

**167**

child to read books or can read books to her that foster values parents want to reinforce. The key is to use the media to encourage critical thought.

## Teaching a Child about Drugs and Alcohol

Today's parents, many of whom tried drugs themselves as teenagers and who are part of the generation that invented wine coolers, may feel hard-pressed to justify their wish that their own kid refrain from experimenting with drugs and alcohol. When a child asks, "Mom, did you ever smoke grass?" parents who *did* are likely to feel somewhat hypocritical when they answer, "Well, yes, but that was different." Likewise, a parent who drinks may feel he isn't standing on firm moral ground when he insists that his child not drink.

If a parent's past or present lifestyle includes drug or alcohol use and/or smoking, he is in the unfortunate position of saying, "Do as I say, not as I do." In terms of the present, parental example will speak the loudest. Parents who abuse drugs are much more likely to have a kid who abuses drugs. Parents who drink *moderately* and *responsibly* have to help their teen realize that the rights and responsibilities of adults are not the same as those of teens.

If parents choose to reveal past experiences, they can answer honestly that they did things in their past that they are not proud of today and relate some of the real harm that came to themselves or to friends as a result of their substance abuse. They can emphasize that having children, loving them, and wanting what's best for them has given them all the reason in the world to disapprove of drug and alcohol use today.

Parents who never tried drugs, cigarettes, or alcohol may

feel an advantage in addressing the issue of substance abuse with their child, but these parents need to make a real effort to understand why the lure of drugs and alcohol is so strong. They also need to examine why their child should choose to do something so out of line with the messages she has received from parental example. What can parents do and say to help their child develop the confidence and internal strength to say no, even when doing so may cause her temporary ridicule or rejection?

Adolescents use and misuse drugs and alcohol for all sorts of reasons. Research shows that substance abusers, be they adults or children, are generally lonely, estranged from others, frustrated with and unable to feel good about themselves, or think no one cares about what they do. Sometimes they indulge to a point of excess as a means of coping with rejection, as a way to win points from their peers, or as a tool for overcoming inhibitions. Some people have a physical tendency toward addiction even after using a small amount of a drug. Substance abuse may also be a deliberate statement of defiance toward parents (''I'll show them they can't stop me from doing whatever I want'') or a way to rebel against society's codes of conduct. And it is often a crutch that allows abusers to escape life's harsh realities. Using and dealing drugs may be seen as an avenue to economic success.

Parents need to take an active role to discourage substance abuse. Drug abuse poses a risk to a teen's physical health, but the emotional ramifications can be even worse. ''Just at the time when a young person is learning to cope and to become responsible, drugs can come in and wipe out success, competence, coping skills, and social relationships,'' writes Barbara Brenner, author of *Love and Discipline*. ''Drugs don't kill the person as much as they kill the full human potential of the person, and no parent wants that to happen to a child.'' It helps if parents' approach to the subject is tempered with reason. If parents respond frantically or adopt a self-righteous posture, they will quickly lose their child's attention. Allowing tempers to erupt, nagging, threatening, making accusations, or giving out harsh punishments are generally ineffective ways to discourage a child from drinking or experimenting with drugs.

Approach the subject, instead, with calmness, empathy, concern, and conviction. "I panicked when I found a small amount of marijuana in Barbara's room," recalls her mother. "I was all set to confront her. Luckily I waited until I had calmed down. Then I asked if we could talk for a few minutes."

During their conversation, Barbara's mother firmly explained how she felt about pot smoking:

*I told her that I knew a lot of other kids were trying marijuana, but that in this family it was definitely not acceptable. I said I didn't want her smoking pot in the house or even bringing it into the house. I let her know how much respect I had for her judgment and I explained why I thought marijuana was detrimental to her physical and mental development. I didn't say "You must never do this again." I did say I hoped she cared enough about herself and her family not to, but that because I couldn't be with her every moment, I couldn't force her not to. I told her that if I found her again with marijuana, I would take it as a sign that she needs help and I would take her to a drug program. She certainly understood that I felt very strongly about the issue.*

Some parents choose to remove the "forbidden" label from alcohol by offering preteens or teens an occasional alcoholic beverage at home. The idea is to reduce the fascination and mystery that liquor often holds. "We let Ron occasionally have a sip of one of our drinks," explained one father. "I'd rather he learn to cope with alcohol at home than feel he has to sneak off with his friends to see what it is all about." Some experts disagree with this approach, however, noting that the earlier a person begins to use alcohol, the more likely he is to become addicted to it. If there is a family history of alcoholism particularly, parents should be wary of allowing children to imbibe because studies show that the tendency toward addiction may have a genetic component.

Here are some other ways to deal with the issue of substance abuse:

- **Fortify yourself with accurate information about drugs and alcohol and use it to educate children.** Most libraries have several recently published books that give the facts on drugs, alcohol, and addiction. A family physician may also be a possible source for information. Parents should try not to make wild claims just to frighten children. Telling a child that marijuana use leads directly to cocaine addiction, for example, will probably destroy parents' credibility once their child learns the truth. However, parents do need to tell the truth about addiction. Many teens who are using drugs and alcohol claim they can quit whenever they feel like it. They are not aware of the dangers of psychological dependency as well as physical dependency. Teens need to know that once someone becomes a user there are no instant cures. Recovery is a long and hard process.
- **Inform children of the legal ramifications of using drugs and alcohol.** Parents need to know what the legal alcohol limit for driving is in their state and the penalities for being caught with a small amount of such drugs as marijuana and cocaine. They can then show their child how little liquid a person can consume to be considered le-

gally drunk, for example, and tell her what happens if she is caught driving while drunk.

- **Be a responsible role model.** Adolescents are acutely sensitive to anything they perceive as hypocrisy and they will tune out adults whose words contradict their actions.

- **Teach children to be critical of misleading role models.** They need to understand that most people who drink do not have as much fun as the people they see in commercials, nor are they that attractive. Children also need to be aware that the athletes and entertainers they idolize do not always excel in every area of their lives. While they are talented people, they are no wiser than other people and are subject to problems with drugs and alcohol.

- **Begin early to talk about appropriate attitudes toward drugs and alcohol.** Children need to know how their parents feel. Youngsters are most open to discussion when they are young, which can help set the stage for continuing dialogue as they reach their touchy teenage years. Parents need to ask direct questions (''Do any of your friends use drugs?'' or ''What would you do if someone offered you a drink?'') and be prepared to listen and discuss their responses, not to judge them.

In *Bringing Up a Moral Child,* Dr. Michael Schulman and Eva Mekler advise: ''From a very young age—when she's six or seven—get her to think about the kind of person she has to be in order to help bring about the kind of world she'd like to live in. Also, point out people whose actions help bring this ideal closer and contrast them with those who make the world an unhappy and cruel place. Among the repugnant people will be those who diminish their ability to lead constructive lives or to give of themselves by overindulging on drugs or alcohol.'' Parents also need to remember that their child is a whole person. Her behavior reflects what kind of a person she is. If generally she cares about others, is honest with herself, and is emotionally secure, she is more likely to resist destructive behavior. Parents can help with this by following these points:

- **Establish curfews and rules about overnight parties for adolescents.** Clear guidelines about when it is okay to visit friends in homes where there is no adult supervision also need to be provided. Parents should try to be consistently firm about these subjects; young adolescents badly need adult guidance, no matter how overtly hostile they may be toward it. In fact they sometimes rely on and are relieved by parental insistence as an excuse to say no to their friends.
- **Teach children how to say no.** This includes talking about situations in which a child might be encouraged to drink or use drugs, such as at a party, before or after school, or at a sporting event, and whether or not she might be made fun of if she refuses. She may need to be taught actual words she could use to say no, including what to say if she is further pressured.
- **Be alert to signs that a child is abusing alcohol or drugs.** Signs might include any puzzling change in behavior, such as sudden hostility or irritability. A child might also become less communicative, drop friends and school activities, begin failing school subjects, and show indifference to things in which she was previously interested. She may be keeping company with new friends who use drugs. Parents also may notice that money is disappearing from around the house, which may point to a child needing to steal to pay for drugs. Parents who know their child's personality should be able to distinguish between normal, teenage mood changes and those caused by drugs or alcohol.

- **Confront problems directly, rather than allow them to remain hidden.** It is easy to avoid real issues of concern, but staying silent in the belief that "she can work it out for herself" is conterproductive. Ignoring it sends a message that says, "I am unable to deal with this problem." A child needs to feel secure that her parents can hold a steady course in rough waters. So parents should insist on candid answers to straightforward questions. Parents also need to resist letting a child con them with pat responses or vague statements, such as "All the other kids do it" or "I can handle it." Parents need to make it clear they will not make excuses to friends, teachers, or family members for a child's behavior. If a child indulges in dangerous habits, she will have to accept the consequences of her own actions. Parents might also have to realize and let their child know that, although they love her, they do not want to live with someone who is a substance abuser, but that they do want her to get help through a recovery program and they will assist her in finding the help she needs.

- **If a child does develop a problem with drinking or drugs, parents need to fight as hard as they can to keep the lines of communication open.** When a child begins to use illegal drugs, she withdraws from close contact with the people who know her best. The more she indulges in forbidden behavior, the greater the wedge that gets driven between parent and child. When she is at her most hostile and becomes hardest to reach, she needs support and help more than ever. She needs to know that her family will do anything they can to get her off drugs and back into a productive life.

If parents suspect a drug or alcohol problem, they should seek help immediately and not be ashamed to do so. Schools often have programs to help parents and students identify a drug problem and supply information on where to go for professional treatment. Parents should find out where they can go for help and make contact with a professional before confronting their child. A parent should also consider not confronting a child alone but doing so with the help of the other spouse, siblings, and possibly a professional. If a child asks for help herself, parents need to move quickly and not waste time on accusations or uncertainty about what to do. Treatment might include regular visits to a doctor and therapist, or perhaps a live-in treatment program if the problem is severe. Many community agencies also deal with drug and alcohol problems. One of the most familiar is Alcoholics Anonymous. Phoenix House and Daytop Village also operate in many communities. Parents also need to realize that a family that has been dealing with a substance abuser often needs help as well. Professional counseling is recommended to assist the family in healing themselves and in learning how to help the abuser recover.

## How Peer Counseling Can Help

Peer counseling also is an effective tool for reaching children before they get into serious trouble. Especially in their teenage years, children are often more comfortable listening to their peers than to even the most sympathetic adults.

A peer counseling program was established at one urban junior high school at the suggestion of a teacher who was concerned about adolescent drinking patterns. One of the counselors was a boy named Paul, who had flunked out of school because he drank too much. He was several years older than most of the other students, which gave him some authority and credibility in their eyes. Yet he used language they understood to talk about issues they could relate to.

''I used to drink a six-pack of beer, sometimes two, after

school almost every day," he told an attentive class of 13-year-olds. "Then I'd come home and sleep it off before my parents got back from work. I never had time for homework, I never had time to go out with girls, I even stopped playing basketball." After hearing Paul describe the path he had traveled—dropping out of school, entering a rehabilitation program, and finally getting his life back on track—one boy said: "He's really been there, he knows what it's like to make a big mistake and pay the price for it. A guy like that really makes me think."

Parents who try to communicate a similar message may not be credible in the eyes of their children. But a teenager who has learned the hard way that drinking and drugs don't represent the best that life has to offer can make a big impression on peers.

## Sexually Speaking

As the bodies of young people mature, sex is very much on their minds. That's healthy and natural. What's of concern to parents is that too many adolescents are acting prematurely and irresponsibly on their thoughts. Social norms have obviously changed markedly over the past few decades, and children are experimenting with sex at younger and younger ages. Children are physically maturing earlier than they once did, too. Because of improved medical care and diet, girls now mature as young as nine, while boys usually mature around the age of 11. By 11 or 12, many children talk a lot about sex and may brag about their exploits, real or imagined. The sad result of early sexual activity can be seen in the soaring rate of teenage pregnancies and in the spread of sexually transmitted diseases, including AIDS, which now represent health problems of serious proportions.

Although moral and religious attitudes toward premarital sex differ, any responsible adult disapproves of sexual activities among young adolescents. The imbalance between a child's physical and emotional maturity can create a lot of confusion during this delicate developmental stage. Rushing into sexual experiences at a young age can even cause later emotional as well as physical problems.

As with drugs and alcohol, there are limits to what parents can do to prevent their children from experimenting with sex. The choice to behave responsibly has to come from within children themselves.

Parents and educators can encourage responsible choices by providing accurate and detailed information about sex. Information from peers or the media is usually misleading, incomplete, and often inaccurate, and studies show that keeping a child uninformed about biological and sexual realities *increases* the likelihood that she will become sexually active and that she will fail to use birth control.

Dr. Haim G. Ginott, in *Between Parent and Teenager*, gave this perceptive answer about whether or not sex education should be offered to teenagers: "This question comes too late. Sex is already being 'taught'—on the screen, in the school yard, and in the streets. Sex education is now needed to serve as an antidote to sex propaganda. Society can no longer passively permit the street and the screen to set its sex standards."

Whether it is offered at home, at church, or in the schools, effective sex education should include accurate information about the body's sexual functions, the right of an individual to her privacy, the obligations for self-respect and respect for others, and an understanding of what intimacy really means. Sex education should also include detailed lessons on the function and use of contraceptives, and knowledge about obtaining them. To be useful, the information must be repeated more than once. Sex education should also address the immediate concerns of today's teenagers, who need the opportunity to talk candidly about their sexual feelings and how to handle them.

While many parents advocate innovative sex education in the schools, others protest it with outspoken anger. They argue that sex is a private matter and that the family or the church are the only appropriate settings in which to explore the subject. Unfortunately, neither institution is doing a very good job of filling the information gap. The best estimates are that only 25 percent of parents provide sex education at home. One reason is that many adults don't know much about the subject themselves. Still other parents mistakenly consider their duty done if they give a onetime explanation of the anatomical differences between boys and girls. Others try to disregard the subject because they find frank discussions about sex embarrassing, especially with their children. They also may feel that sex education encourages promiscuity and that talking about birth control is equivalent to advocating teenage sex. However, knowledge of the emotional, moral, and physical consequences of sex is every child's right. Many children want real reasons they can use confidently for refusing to do something they don't want to do. And if a teenager is determined to have sex, at least she can be aware of how to do so responsibly.

As with drugs, a young person's self-esteem has a lot to do with whether or not she feels comfortable refraining from sexual activity when she doesn't want it. Peer pressure can often be intense. Saying no when everyone around her seems to be saying yes requires a lot of internal confidence. Adolescents who feel good about themselves are less likely to think they have to prove something and are not as hungry to gain acceptance from the in crowd through sexual activity. As one perceptive teenager observed, ''I think the unpopular people are the ones having sex because they need the love.''

It is not uncommon for parents to discover sexually explicit magazines or photographs in the rooms of their preadolescent and teenage children, especially boys. Usually this reflects a child's intense curiosity and is not a sign that anything is wrong. Most parents, no matter how liberal they are in their thinking, experience some shock at seeing their own child with sexual pictures. If parents have not had many candid conversations about sex with their child, they can take their discovery as a clue that she is looking for accurate information. Instead of punishing her for her curiosity, it is probably time her parents talked with her about sex.

Parents need to accept their obligation to help their child understand her own sexuality and feel comfortable with it. Becoming at ease with her own body is a process that begins in infancy and requires a foundation of knowledge that should be built upon during the preteen years. Young children can be taught accurate names for genitals and their function in age-appropriate terms. They also need to learn to value and respect their own and others' bodies and to know they have a right to refuse any kind of intimate contact if they don't want it. Helping to provide a healthy acceptance of sexuality lays a foundation that allows children to move more smoothly through adolescence and sets the stage for responsible sexual behavior throughout life.

Initiate conversations about sexuality and reproduction periodically, rather than on a single momentous occasion. If parents have talked with children about sexuality early on, these conversations will be fairly easy to initiate with a grade-schooler. If parents have not previously talked about sex, they might look for a natural opening, such as a reference to something in a television show or at the event of a birth in the family. However, parents should not wait until a child asks a question. She may never ask, or already have a great deal of misinformation by the time she does.

By kindergarten age a child may begin to ask some basic questions, such as "Where did I come from?" By nine or 10 she may have heard talk about AIDS or abortion and want to know what the words mean. As she nears puberty, anywhere from nine to 13, she is probably hearing a lot of talk about sex from her friends. Much of it is probably inaccurate—one more reason why she needs to be fully armed with facts.

Before answering their child's questions or beginning a conversation about sex, parents need to try to ascertain what the child already knows or really wants to know at the time. This will give them some idea of where to start and what misinformation needs to be corrected. There are several books available in the library that help parents address the topic for different age levels.

Parents should present information accurately, but not in strictly clinical terms. They should explore the emotional dimensions of sexuality as well, in age-appropriate language. As the Planned Parenthood guide *How to Talk With Your Child About Sexuality* says, "Giving young children the information they need about sexual development is relatively simple. Their questions are usually quite matter-of-fact and can be answered in that spirit. They dote on facts. Teenagers, on the other hand, would like to ask their parents much more complicated questions. They are deeply preoccupied with finding out who they are and what their relationships with other people should be."

One approach parents should avoid is trying to be too much of a pal to a child when talking about sex. The last thing she needs is more jocular or careless talk, which is what she probably gets from peers who don't really understand the subject. Instead, let her know that sex should be taken seriously. Let her know that sex is one very important form of communication between people who love each other and that it is something to be shared only with someone very special.

Clearly expressing feelings about teenage sex is important. Some parents are so concerned about being called old-fashioned that they hesitate to express any opinions at all. A better approach is for parents to state their point of view in a nonjudgmental way, and to talk about the genuine physical and social risks of pregnancy and disease for young people, as well as the emotional complications of sex.

One unusual program at an urban high school that dramatized the responsibilities of having a baby showed how imaginative education can emphasize the consequences of unprotected sex. For two weeks, teenagers in one teacher's classroom were assigned to carry around a 20-pound sack of flour wherever they went, even if they were just dashing to the store. When they wished to spend an evening alone, baby-sitting arrangements had to be made. Occasionally, the teacher spot-checked his students, calling them at home or even dropping by for an unannounced visit to be certain they were meeting their obligations to the sack of flour. There was a lot of grumbling about the assignment, but at the end of the two-week period, most of the students agreed that they had a much clearer understanding of what it means to care for an infant.

Parents should not be afraid to set limits. Faced by the temptations of their age, most children need to have limits set for them, not the opportunity to do whatever they want. However, parents must first decide what they will and will not allow. Restrictions may include not allowing a daughter to have her boyfriend in the bedroom with the door closed, not allowing weekend trips without adult chaperones, and making sure that parents meet a boy or a girl their child may be dating.

Trying to prevent a child from having sex may, however,

prove fruitless. Dr. Schulman and Mekler write, "Many teens view parental injunctions against sex as simply an instance of one generation trying to impose its sexual conventions on another. It may feel like a moral issue to an adult who was brought up to believe that sex outside of marriage is sinful or dirty, but it's hard to convince today's teenagers of this." They do recommend teaching children to treat boyfriends and girlfriends sensitively: "Teach them not to think of sexual intimacy as *taking* but as *sharing*. Sharing means that you regard the other person as a whole person—not just as something for your enjoyment. When you treat someone as a whole person you must consider his or her feelings and goals and fears and what the consequences of your actions will be for him or her."

Besides being available to talk about aspects of intercourse, parents also need to be askable about all the other aspects of sex between first attraction and actual intercourse. Many children worry about and want reassurance and guidance on their fantasies, impulses, feelings of awkwardness, and specific body changes they are going through. Girls are often not prepared for feelings of moodiness and the sudden onset of bleeding when menstruation begins. Boys may be embarrassed about wet dreams and want to know what causes them. Another child may want to know why she feels physically tingly at the thought of holding someone's hand or being kissed and what to do with these feelings. Reassure children that these feelings are okay. If a child talks about "really liking the new boy in class," don't criticize her for it. Let her know that sexual attraction is a natural part of growing up but that just because she likes someone, and may even dream of kissing and touching him, this doesn't mean that she has to act on it. Often children are relieved when they are told it is okay *not* to have sex. Parents can say, "It's exciting to meet someone you really like. Every friend is special. You can be very close to someone emotionally without having to be physically intimate." Children can also be told the benefits of waiting to have sex until they are more emotionally mature.

Some parents may find that their child refuses to talk about sex. This also is a common situation. In *Raising a Child Conservatively in a Sexually Permissive World*, Sol Gordon, Ph.D., and Judith Gordon recommend, "Plan ahead; have a book ready. Tell your son that you think he might be interested in it. Explain that some of the material might embarrass him, but that you're going to leave the book around just the same. The main thing is for him to understand that you are available to talk anytime he is ready."

Parents also need to be ready to help a child through the emotional ups and downs of relationships. Whether or not a teenager has been sexually intimate with a boyfriend or girlfriend, many relationships come to an end, often painfully. Part of the hard part of growing up is learning that even a loving relationship can end because feelings change, or someone moves away or meets someone else. Accepting and recovering from the loss is difficult. Parents need to be ready to leave their child alone for a while, if necessary, and make themselves available to talk. They can try to help their child understand that what's important is that she is lovable and a worthwhile person, no matter whether she is in a relationship or not. Such reassurances may seemingly fall on deaf ears, but a child does need to hear that she will survive and find someone else in time.

Sometimes parents inadvertently lead a child to drug or alcohol abuse or to premature sexual activity. Concerned that their child should be popular, they arrange for boy-girl parties for 10-year-olds—parties that would be more appropriate for teens. They let their teens have a beer party so that their child won't feel left out, or they let her date before she is ready and when group activities would be more appropriate.

## Making a Difference in the World

The nature of teenagers means that they often approach all segments of life with varying and extreme degrees of enthusiasm, idealism, uncertainty, passion, conviction, egotism, and seriousness. Their impulsiveness sometimes leads them to experiments with drugs, alcohol, and sex because of a lack of any other direction. Or it can lead them into making a real contribution to the world around them.

As a child becomes increasingly independent and mobile, she learns more about what lies beyond the boundaries of her immediate environment. She also takes notice of the injustice that is all around her. The harsh signs of poverty and homelessness, for example, are too visible to ignore, especially in urban areas. A child can also see the scars left on the planet by environmental disasters and human carelessness. And all along she is likely to have heard nasty remarks made about people from differing ethnic, racial, or religious backgrounds.

A confident and compassionate adolescent can be more than a passive bystander who observes these events but feels powerless to do anything about them. There is nothing more demoralizing than looking at a troubled world and thinking, ''There's nothing I can do to make things better.'' Instead, parents hope their children will ask, ''What can I do to make a difference? How can I help?'' A key dimension of behaving responsibly, then, is being guided by conscience and trying to meet the obligations of being wholly human. As one father said, ''To me, being a responsible adult means doing more than just going to work, coming home, and taking care of your family. It means thinking in a broader sense about the world at large and getting involved in the community.''

More than 30 years ago, President John F. Kennedy stirred the nation by his moving and timeless plea (updated from a speech given by Oliver Wendell Holmes in 1884), ''Ask not what your country can do for you; ask what you can do for your country.'' Such a sentiment is as valid today as when it was first uttered.

## Inspiring Commitment in Your Children

The fact is that our society badly needs their time and energy. In *New Roles for Youth in the School and the Community*, a report by the National Commission on Resources for Youth, the authors conclude: ''The unmet needs in our society are so great that there should be a place for any young person who wants to make a contribution. Equally important, a young person's need to be needed cannot long be ignored without significant loss to his self-esteem and to his present and future achievement and personal satisfaction.''

Children can be encouraged to become involved in the life of their community by talking to them about the complex moral and political issues facing our society today. Unless children are well informed, they will not have the motivation to struggle for change. Peer discussion groups, organized through the schools, the church, or a community agency, are one good way for children to learn more. For example, a group of preteens and teens in Detroit took a tour of a city shelter after meeting in a church basement to discuss the roots of homelessness. Donna, 12, was so moved by her experience that she helped organize a clothing drive at her school. Within a month, two carloads of donated goods had been delivered to the shelter she had visited.

Parents can also call attention to important issues in newspaper and magazine articles, and on television news broadcasts. Many teenagers might show little interest in larger issues, but parents may eventually stumble on a topic that inspires them to get involved. Often it happens when someone they know becomes involved in something or is personally affected by an issue, such as sexual or racial discrimination, a neighborhood environmental problem, or work layoffs.

Teaching a child to respect racial and religious differences among people is also important. American society has always been composed of many languages and cultures, and no child can make a real contribution unless she is tolerant of other people's differences and is relatively free of prejudice and mistrust. The way parents themselves treat people from backgrounds other than their own also provides a child with her most important model of tolerance.

Children can be told or shown stories about people who were guided by their conscience rather than the hope of reward. For example, parents might clip newspaper articles about individuals who stood up for what they believed. The civilian who stepped forward to stop a robbery in progress, the teacher who organized a fund-raising drive to save the rain forest, the nine-year-old who collected and distributed blankets to street people, the group of young professionals in Atlanta who built shelters for the homeless, and the politician who took the risk of speaking out against a policy popular with his constituency are all examples of people who cared enough to make a contribution instead of saying "Let someone else do it."

Parents can set a good example. They can begin by remembering that small steps do matter. Whether parents are doing some volunteer work once a week, studying the roots of poverty and injustice, or donating to a charity of their choice, they can show their children that parents, like everyone, have a role to play in changing the world. Parents can also talk enthusiastically about their work. One father explained his political activities by saying, ''I'm setting up a telephone tree by asking five friends to call five other friends. If all of them agree to call their state senators and ask them to vote for more funds for the school system, we can really have an impact.''

Finally, parents can help children find ways to make their mark. Adolescents are sometimes criticized for being self-centered, but experience shows they welcome the opportunity to play a meaningful role in socially relevant projects.

## The Value of Volunteer Service

For parents who wonder whether or not their teenagers should be working part-time, an alternative might be to encourage them to find volunteer activities suitable to their interests. Like working for pay, volunteer service increases a child's independence, teaches discipline, and helps her develop a sense of competence.

Volunteering has other dimensions as well. For one thing, it exposes children, especially those who have grown up in privileged environments, to the problems of others. One teenager who served as a Big Brother to a mildly disabled youngster living in an disadvantaged neighborhood commented, ''After seeing how overcrowded his apartment was, I realized that I was lucky to grow up in a big house with a backyard and lots of room. I'd never much thought about it before because everyone I went to school with lived in comfortable houses, like me.''

Volunteer service can also teach patience and compassion. It can be empowering because it provides young people tangible evidence that their skills and energies can make a real difference in the lives of others. It also provides a lesson in good citizenship, teaching a child to look beyond her immediate circle of friends and family toward her role as a functioning member of a larger society.

The National Commission on Resources for Youth found that the most successful projects "have one overriding characteristic—they offer a young person a type of participation that demands responsible action on his part, provide him with opportunities to make decisions that affect himself and others, and let him experience the consequences of his own actions and decisions. Good projects also have a common goal—they all aim to help young people grow, achieve, and develop positive attitudes toward themselves as participants in the adult world."

Many volunteer opportunities are open to junior high and high school children. Along with the social and educational functions they serve, Girl Scout and Boy Scout troops often emphasize service. It is not uncommon for a scout troop to spend one day a week visiting senior citizens in a recreational center or playing with developmentally disabled children at a special school. Adolescents also have been engaged to rebuild eroded trails in rural Maine, to clean up polluted beaches in southern Florida, and to tutor children with academic problems in New York. Other good sources for volunteer opportunities are local hospitals, which frequently have Candy Striper programs; homeless shelters; humane societies; city parks; recreation departments; church organizations; and programs for disadvantaged children.

"Until I started working with children at a rehabilitation hospital, I was mostly interested in clothing and boys," says 12-year-old Jeanine. "I guess I still am, but now there's a whole lot more going on in my life. When I see a little girl playing a game or using a skill I taught her I feel as if what I'm doing really counts. Sometimes I think these kids are

teaching me as much as I'm teaching them. They're showing me how we all matter to each other.''

# A Final Word

Raising a responsible child is a highly complex task, but
most parents do find that they are successful at it. The key
is to assemble the building blocks. A child with a strong
sense of self-esteem, the capacity to empathize, an understanding of the difference between right and wrong, confidence in her own judgment, and a grasp of the
consequences of her actions has the best chance to flower
into responsible adulthood.

Chances are that if parents model appropriate behavior,
their child will eventually learn to imitate it. But parents
should not feel guilty or anxious when they make a mistake. Even if they know, in theory, that it is better to provide constructive feedback than to criticize angrily, parents
*will* lose their temper at times. If parents acknowledge their
slipups and use them as a tool to let their child know it is
normal to make mistakes, they will have taught another
enduring lesson.

One final reminder: Parents need to define their notion
of responsibility broadly. While loyalty to friends and family and commitment to their jobs are necessary parts of the
package, parents should not restrict their child's vision of
the world to their own. A child who is raised responsibly
will find her own vision, and it will be one that empowers
her, enables her, and gives her hope.

● ● ● ● ● ● ● ● ● ● ● ● ● ● ● ● ● ● ● ● ● ● ● ● ● ● ● ● ● ● ●

## Kids ask:

*I'm what they call a virgin on the verge. I'm 17 and as far as I know I'm the only girl who hasn't yet had sex. I know that having sex now goes against everything my parents want for me. But my boyfriend and I will be careful. We both plan to use birth control. Why should I wait when no one else has?*

Contrary to this teenager's perceptions, not everyone is having sex. Less than half of high school-age teenagers have sex before they graduate. However, when teenagers decide to become sexually active, there is little parents can do to stop them. Before becoming involved, teens should, however, consider some basic questions: Is this someone I really love and whom I want to be with after we have sex? Is this really a friend I can talk with, rather than just someone to have sex with? Do I want to do this secretly or with my parents' knowledge? In addition, teens need to know that using birth control is not enough. They must also consider whether they know all they need to know about safer sex. One reminder: Sex is more than just an act. It's part of a whole relationship with another person. It's something that people should save for those they care about.

# Resources

· · · · · ·

## Organizations

*Association for the Care of Children's Health (ACCH)*, 3615 Washington Avenue N.W., Washington, DC 20016    (202) 244-1801

This organization of health-care workers, educators, and parents is devoted to improving the ways in which health-care professionals respond to the unique emotional and developmental needs of children. It is committed to humanizing medical care for children and their families. The association publishes books and films for adults and children.

*Association for Childhood Education International (ACEI)*, 1141 Georgia Avenue, Suite 200, Wheaton, MD 20902    (301) 942-2443

ACEI's main purpose is to focus the attention of the public on the educational needs and inherent rights of children, as well as programs for their well-being. Members work to raise standards for those involved with the care and development of children. It publishes the internationally acclaimed semiannual journal *Childhood Education*.

*Carnegie Council on Adolescent Development*, 11 Du Pont Circle N.W., Washington, DC 20036    (202) 265-9080

The Carnegie Council of New York established the Carnegie Council on Adolescent Development to place the challenges of adolescent years higher on the nation's agenda. The council generates public and private support for measures that facilitate the critical transition into adulthood. It conducts the Task Force on the Education of Young Adolescents, which is engaged in a wide-ranging examination of current educational experiences of young adolescents.

*Institute for American Values (IAV)*, 250 West 57th Street, Suite 2415, New York, NY 10107    (212) 246–3942

The institute is a nonprofit, nonpartisan organization concerned with issues affecting the American family. Its principal purpose is to deliver to the media timely and useful research on family issues. It seeks to bring family concerns into the mainstream of national policy debate. A biannual publication entitled *Family Affairs* is available.

*National Association on Drug Abuse Problems (NADAP)*, 355 Lexington Avenue, New York, NY 10017    (212) 986–1170

NADAP is a private, nonprofit organization dedicated to fighting drug and alcohol abuse in the family, the community, and the workplace. It works toward fulfilling the right of every individual to live and work in an environment free from drug and alcohol abuse.

*National Association for the Education of Young Children (NAEYC)*, 1834 Connecticut Avenue N.W., Washington, DC 20009
(202) 212–8777

This organization provides educational resources for adults who are committed to improving the quality and availability of services for children from birth through age eight. There are more than 72,000 members and 400 local, state, and regional affiliate groups. Publications include pamphlets and brochures, such as "How to Choose a Good Early Childhood Program," and a journal for members, entitled *Young Children*.

*National Committee for Citizens in Education (NCCE)*, 10840 Little Patuxent Parkway, Columbia, MD 21044    (301) 787–0977

NCCE is a citizen-advocacy group for public education, devoted to improving the quality of public schools through increased public involvement. It provides the information resources parents and other citizens need to become involved in school decision making at the local level. It also has a program that trains parents and educators to work together constructively. Services include a computerized clearinghouse of school-related information for parents who call their toll-free hot line; a direct-mail catalog carrying many publications focused on public involvement; and a monthly newsletter, entitled *Network*.

*National Dropout Prevention Center*, Clemson University, Clemson, SC 29634    (803) 656-2599

The National Dropout Prevention Center's mission is to reduce significantly the dropout rate in American schools. It is committed to a comprehensive and systematic approach that ensures that all youth receive the quality education to which they are entitled. The center works toward its goal through efforts in public policy and educational practice. It publishes a quarterly newsletter.

*National Parents' Resource Institute for Drug Education, Inc. (PRIDE)*, Hurt Building, Suite 210, 50 Hurt Plaza, Atlanta, GA 30303    (404) 577-4500

PRIDE is dedicated to preventing drug and alcohol use by adolescents. It offers a range of programs and services to parents, youth, community organizers, and educators. These include the PRIDE questionnaire for grades 6-12, which allows communities to monitor drug abuse among their youth; a training workshop for parents; and a network linking parents to resources in any region of the nation. It also publishes a quarterly newsletter, *The PRIDE Quarterly*.

*National PTA—National Congress of Parents and Teachers*, 700 North Rush, Chicago, IL 60611    (312) 787-0977

This child-advocacy association is dedicated to the health, education, and safety of children and teens. It has more than 26,000 local chapters and 6.4 million members. A national convention is held annually. Publications include inexpensive booklets and monographs, filmstrips, recordings, and posters on many aspects of education; the prize-winning magazine *PTA Today*; and a newsletter, *What's Happening in Washington*.

# Books for Adults

Bernstein, Joanne E., and Marsha K. Rudman. *Books to Help Children Cope with Separation and Loss: An Annotated Bibliography*, Vol. 3. New York: Bowker, 1988.

This excellent essay on how books help children cope with a variety of life situations provides an extensive annotated list of titles and is well indexed and easy to use.

Bombeck, Erma. *Family: The Ties That Bind . . . and Gag!* New York: McGraw-Hill, 1987.

A family reunion sets the stage for Erma Bombeck's hilarious recollections of raising a family. This is an entertaining and insightful look at American family life over the last two decades.

Bombeck, Erma. *"Just Wait Till You Have Children of Your Own!"* Illustrated by Bil Keane. Garden City, N.Y.: Doubleday, 1971.

Two of America's foremost family humorists look at teenagers. A warm and lighthearted account of family life with teens.

Brazelton, T. Berry, M.D. *Toddlers and Parents: A Declaration of Independence.* New York: Delacorte Press, 1974.

Dr. Brazelton provides a comprehensive explanation of the changes young children experience between the ages of one and 2½. He gives reassuring advice on how to deal with such issues as negativism and fear of separation. He also addresses the special problems of single parents, working parents, and large families.

Briggs, Dorothy Corkille. *Your Child's Self-Esteem: Step-by-Step Guidelines for Raising Responsible, Productive, Happy Children: The Key to His Life.* Garden City, N.Y.: Doubleday, 1975.

Briggs believes self-esteem gives children the strength to meet stress and the courage to become committed, responsible, productive, creative, and humane adults. This calm, sensitive approach to child rearing offers suggestions on how to create strong feelings of self-worth in your child.

Butler, Dorothy. *Babies Need Books*. New York: Atheneum, 1980.

This inspirational and practical book gives sound advice on the importance of books and literature to the raising of caring and competent human beings.

Children's Television Workshop. Written by Mary Lee Grisanti, Dian G. Smith, and Charles Flatter, Ph.D. *Parents' Guide to Understanding Discipline: Infancy Through Preteen*. New York: Prentice Hall Press, 1990.

Presents information on child development and strategies for child rearing and discipline. Grounded in current research, it offers useful advice with practical suggestions on how to raise children with loving firmness. An excellent guide and part of the CTW Family Living Series, with an introduction by Lawrence Balter, Ph.D.

Colby, Anne, and Lawrence Kohlberg. *The Measurement of Moral Judgment*. 2 vols. New York: Cambridge University Press, 1987.

This two-volume set constitutes the definitive presentation of the system of classifying moral judgment built up by Lawrence Kohlberg and his associates over a period of 20 years.

Coles, Robert, M.D. *The Call of Stories: Teaching and the Moral Imagination*. Boston: Houghton Mifflin, 1989.

Coles discusses the moral insights that come from stories and books, beginning with those that are read aloud in the family circle and continuing through formal education and beyond. He contends that much of our moral understanding comes from traditional sources, such as religion and literature.

Coles, Robert, M.D. *The Moral Life of Children*. Boston: Atlantic Monthly Press, 1986.

Leading psychiatrist and author Robert Coles explores the moral reactions of children of various backgrounds to life depicted in movies, as well as at home, school, and in the street. In a compelling and compassionate study, he marvels at the intense moral awareness of some children and ponders its source.

Cosby, Bill, Ed.D. *Fatherhood*. Garden City, N.Y.: Doubleday, 1986.

A wise and witty collection of anecdotes, vignettes, and musings about fatherhood. From his perspective as son and father, Cosby has written a celebration of parenthood. A manual for prospective fathers and an illuminating guide for wives.

Cutright, Melitta J., Ph.D. *The National PTA Talks to Parents: How to Get the Best Education for Your Child*. New York: Doubleday, 1989.

Clear, sensible, and practical advice, including preparing your child for kindergarten, recognizing good teachers and effective schools, responding to "lemons," and helping with homework.

Demos, John P. *Past, Present, and Personal: The Family and the Life Course in American History*. New York: Oxford University Press, 1988.

This fascinating history of the American family explores differences and similarities in family life, child-rearing practices, adolescence, middle age, the role of the father, and the relevance of the past to today's policy-making processes.

Dinkmeyer, Don, and Gary D. McKay. *Raising a Responsible Child: Practical Steps to Successful Family Relationships*. New York: Simon & Schuster, 1982.

Specific, family-centered egalitarian methods of discipline to benefit the entire family and to create a healthful environment for growth.

Faber, Adele, and Elaine Mazlish. *Siblings Without Rivalry: How to Help Your Children Live Together So You Can Live Too*. New York: Avon Books, 1988.

Based on their parent workshops, the authors offer advice and techniques on how to resolve the conflicts that arise among siblings. Written in a humorous, easy-to-understand style with several anecdotes and personal stories.

Forisha, Bill E., Ph.D., and Penelope B. Grenoble, Ph.D. *Creating a Good Self-Image in Your Child*. Chicago: Contemporary Books, 1988.

Chronological discussion of developmental stages and how they relate to self-image, as well as advice on how to help your child maximize the positive qualities. The authors emphasize the importance of feeling lovable and worthwhile.

Fox, Matthew. *Original Blessing: A Primer in Creation Spirituality Presented in Four Paths, Twenty-six Themes, and Two Questions*. Santa Fe: Bear & Company, 1983.

Dominican scholar and innovative educator Fox attempts to reunite science and religion as compatible pathways to wisdom. He considers creation-centered traditions, such as those of Native Americans, as paradigms for religion that can empower people with a sense of their own creativity and mystic center.

Fraiberg, Selma H. *The Magic Years: Understanding and Handling the Problems of Early Childhood*. New York: Scribner's, 1984.

The inner workings of the mind and emotions of children from birth to six years are described with warmth and perception. Provides insight into dealing with issues of discipline and self-control.

Gerard, Patty Carmichael, and Marian Cohn. *Teaching Your Child Basic Body Confidence*. Boston: Houghton Mifflin, 1988.

The Gerard Method for enhancing physical development through creative play for children up to six years old. It asserts physical self-assurance as the basis of self-confidence and self-reliance.

Gilligan, Carol. *In a Different Voice: Psychological Theory and Women's Development*. Cambridge: Harvard University Press, 1982.

Gilligan looks at the differences in moral development between men and women. She suggests the need to look at women and their psychological development in order to appreciate moral differences rather than accept the notion of female inferiority. She emphasizes the centrality of individuation to the male concept of morality. She asserts that the female concept of moral problems arises from conflicting responsibilities and that it requires different solutions than the male-defined dilemmas of competing rights.

Ginott, Haim G, Ph.D., *Between Parent and Child.* New York: Avon Books, 1976.

This book emphasizes the need for skillful, caring communication with children. Written with compassion and humor by the lates renowned child psychologist.

Ginott, Haim G, Ph.D. *Between Parent and Teenager.* New York: Avon Books, 1982.

Specific advice and strategies for handling the endless series of crises and events that are part of parent-teenager relationships. Insightful, humane guidance on how to listen and talk with your children and how to live with mutual respect and dignity.

Gordon, Sol, Ph.D., and Judith Gordon. *Raising a Child Conservatively in a Sexually Permissive World.* New York: Simon & Schuster, 1989.

Clear-minded, reassuring, and helpful advice by leading educators in the field on what, when, and how much to tell children and teens about sex in order to help them grow into responsible, self-possessed adults.

Gordon, Thomas, Ph.D. *P.E.T., Parent Effectiveness Training: The Tested New Way to Raise Responsible Children.* New York: New American Library, 1988.

A structured method of open-ended dialoguing and discussion to promote less fighting, fewer tantrums, closer and warmer relationships, and more responsible children.

Gurian, Anita, and Ruth Formanek. *The Socially Competent Child: A Parent's Guide to Social Development—From Infancy to Early Adolescence.* Boston: Houghton Mifflin, 1983.

How parents can help their children develop a concern for others while maintaining their own rights. Includes topics such as friendship, moral judgments, manners, and troubled times.

Heffner, Elaine , Ed.D. *Mothering: The Emotional Experience of Motherhood After Freud and Feminism.* Garden City, N.Y.: Doubleday, 1978.

Dr. Heffner discusses the impact of psychoanalytic and feminist theories on motherhood: the first, having added responsibility for emotionally healthy children to the mother's role; the second, having attempted to liberate women from the mothering role without helping them to succeed in it. Dr. Heffner advocates mothering as a "professional choice."

Hoover, Mary B. *The Responsive Parent: Meeting the Realities of Parenthood Today.* New York: Parents' Magazine Press, 1972.
A warm and reassuring book on how to find your own satisfying parenting style while meeting the demands of raising healthy children.

Jenkins, Gladys Gardner, Helen S. Shacter, and William W. Bauer. *These Are Your Children.* 4th ed. Glenview, Ill.: Scott Foresman, 1975.
Revision of the classic work on child development. In this practical, readable guide for parents and teachers, the authors discuss physical, mental, social, and emotional growth, pointing out patterns and differences.

Kagan, Jerome. *The Nature of the Child.* New York: Basic Books, 1984.
World-famous psychologist Kagan challenges the view that moral development is based on reasoning. He argues that moral sense arises out of feelings and that children are biologically prepared to acquire standards. He also argues that humans have a lifelong capacity to change and that early childhood experiences are continually transformed by later events.

Kaplan, Louise J., Ph.D. *Adolescence: The Farewell to Childhood.* New York: Simon & Schuster, 1984.
In this remarkable and moving book, Kaplan elucidates and illuminates the psychological transformations that accompany the physical changes of adolescence. She explains the significance of adolescents' separation from and sadness for the passionate attachments they once felt in childhood toward parents who can no longer be perceived as perfect.

Kozol, Jonathan. *On Being a Teacher.* New York: Continuum, 1981.

National Book Award–winner, educator, and educational critic Kozol once again tackles the system in an effort to challenge public schools and encourage their renewal. He advocates an educational approach that is infused with ethical values and offers suggestions on how teachers, parents, and students can work together toward this end.

Lickona, Thomas, Ph.D. *Raising Good Children: Helping Your Child Through the Stages of Moral Development.* New York: Bantam, 1985.

This book offers practical advice and real-life examples of how to handle discipline issues to instill honesty, courtesy, helpfulness, and respect for others. It also discusses research and explains stages of moral development.

Lightfoot, Sara Lawrence., Ph.D. *The Good High School: Portraits of Character and Culture.* New York: Basic Books, 1985.

What makes a good school? Prominent Harvard educator Dr. Lightfoot addresses this question with an in-depth look at six schools distinguished for excellence. This 1984 winner of the American Educational Research Association Award looks at principals, faculties, students, teaching styles, and the influences of a school's atmosphere on its students' experiences. An insightful exploration of American high school life.

Long, Lynette, Ph.D., and Thomas Long, Ed.D. *The Handbook for Latchkey Children and Their Parents.* New York: Arbor House, 1983.

A practical, down-to-earth guide for working parents and their children that offers realistic and workable solutions for common problems and potential dangers. Topics include learning basic emergency care, alleviating the fears of being alone, getting homework help without parents, and encouraging independence.

Miller, Alice. *For Your Own Good: Hidden Cruelty in Child-Rearing and the Roots of Violence.* New York: Farrar, Straus & Giroux, 1983.

Translated from German, this ground-breaking study of the origins of violence is shattering, frightening, convincing, illuminating, and thought provoking. It focuses on the idea of parents punishing their children for the painful actions of their own parents, in a form of "repetition compulsion." Dr. Miller stresses the need to acknowledge childhood sufferings "lest we pass them on unconsciously to the next generation." Written in a clear, engaging style.

Miller, Alice. *Thou Shalt Not Be Aware: Society's Betrayal of the Child.* New York: New American Library, 1986.

One of the world's foremost psychoanalysts, Dr. Miller exposes the hidden cruelties in the way we raise children, and she shows how abusive treatment of children can lead to destructive consequences, for both the individual and society, such as the development of neuroses, psychic disorders, delinquency, and even violent crime. A compelling, compassionate, and convincing book.

Moe, Harold, and Sandy Moe. *Teach Your Child the Value of Money.* Holmen, Wis.: Harsand Financial Press, 1987.

This book offers advice on how to help your child learn to make thoughtful decisions about money early and how to motivate your child toward a financially successful future.

Mogal, Doris P. *Character in the Making: The Many Ways Parents Can Help the School-Age Child.* New York: Parents' Magazine Press, 1972.

Sensitive and sensible observations and advice about school-age children, their confrontations with the world beyond the family, and the impact of these confrontations on the family. Discusses drugs, television, movies, sex education, prejudice, and the need for new kinds of guidance and reinforcement at home.

Planned Parenthood Federation of America, Inc. *How to Talk With Your Child About Sexuality.* Garden City, N.Y.: Doubleday, 1986.

Practical, comprehensive, no-nonsense guide to helping parents deal intelligently and comfortably with their children's questions about sex and relationships.

Rogers, Fred, and Barry Head. *Mister Rogers Talks with Parents.* New York: Berkley Publishing, 1985.

This book by television's respected expert on children is a compassionate, commonsense approach to how to cope with everyday problems and how to make family life and child rearing as rewarding as possible.

Schulman, Michael, Ph.D., and Eva Mekler. *Bringing Up a Moral Child: A New Approach for Teaching Your Child to Be Kind, Just, and Responsible.* Reading, Mass.: Addison-Wesley, 1985.

Sound, research-based "how-to" manual that not only advises but also explains moral development and the growth of conscience.

Schwebel, Andrew, Ph.D., et al. *A Guide to a Happier Family: Overcoming the Anger, Frustration, and Boredom That Destroy Family Life.* Los Angeles: Jeremy P. Tarcher, 1989.

Written by a family of therapists, this book offers specific, practical guidelines for improving family relationships, along with techniques and scripts on how to enhance communication and empathy.

Sobol, Tom, Ph.D., and Harriet Sobol. *Your Child in School: The Intermediate Years, Grades 3-5.* Vol. 2. New York: Arbor House, 1987.

One of four volumes covering kindergarten through high school, this book details what to expect from your child's school, how to help your child get the most out of it, and what to do if something goes wrong. The Sobols address social as well as educational aspects of school. He is the commissioner of education of New York State, and she is an educator and author of children's books.

Stern, Daniel N., M.D. *The Interpersonal World of the Infant: A View from Psychoanalysis and Developmental Psychology.* New York: Basic Books, 1985.

Infant psychiatrist Stern discusses how babies experience the world around them. He challenges the traditional theories of developmental sequence and the idea that certain states such as attachment, trust, and dependency are restricted to infancy.

Tronick, Edward, Ph.D., and Lauren Adamson, Ph.D. *Babies as People: New Findings on Our Social Beginnings.* New York: Collier, 1980.

The authors demonstrate that babies do not come into the world as simple, passive creatures; instead they "arrive eager and able to perceive and act, to rivet our attention and respond to us in social ways, to express their own uniqueness and mesh with ours."

White, Burton L. *Educating the Infant and Toddler.* Lexington, Mass.: Lexington Books, 1987.

Authoritative and readable, this book by the renowned researcher provides reliable, practical information on what is and is not known about the learning process and developmental stages of young children.

Young, Elaine, with Robert D. Frelow, Ph.D. *I Am a Blade of Grass: A Breakthrough in Learning and Self-Esteem.* Rolling Hills Estates, Calif.: Jalmar Press, 1989.

This inspirational manual discusses how to listen to students and translate their interests into a unified, exciting curriculum that empowers them to become "lifetime learners" with confidence and self-esteem to make a positive difference in their world.

# Books for Children

Ancona, George. *Helping Out.* New York: Clarion Books, 1985.

An exploration in black-and-white photographs of the pleasures and special relationships of adults and children working together. (Ages 3–7)

Anno, Mitsumasa. *Anno's Medieval World.* Adapted from the translation by Ursula Synge. New York: Philomel Books, 1980.

This elegantly crafted book presents an episode in the history of ideas for children. It challenges readers to think about how ideas take hold of a society, how they grow and change. It asks the reader to think about the human cost for these ideas and to appreciate the suffering of the people who struggled to give life to new ideas. (Ages 7 and up)

Bang, Molly. *The Paper Crane.* New York: Greenwillow Books, 1985.
Inventive paper cutouts delight the eye, and spare, elegant prose rewards the ear in this contemporary folktale of a paper crane that comes to life and brings good fortune to a kind man. (Ages 5–8)

Bauer, Marion Dane. *On My Honor.* New York: Clarion Books, 1986.
On a dare, Joel goes swimming in a forbidden river with his best friend, Tony. When Tony drowns, Joel is devastated and terrified at the thought of telling either set of parents what happened. This short, but powerfully gripping novel is a Newbery Medal book. (Ages 10–14)

Berenstain, Stan, and Jan Berenstain. *The Berenstain Bears Forget Their Manners.* New York: Random House, 1985.
Mama Bear comes up with a plan to correct the Bear family's rude behavior. (Ages 3–8)

Berenstain, Stan, and Jan Berenstain. *The Berenstain Bears Get the Gimmies.* New York: Random House, 1988.
Gran and Gramps Bear come up with a plan to rid the cubs of their greediness. (Ages 3–8)

Browne, Anthony. *Piggybook.* New York: Alfred A. Knopf, 1986.
One day overworked Mrs. Piggott walks out on her husband and sons, declaring "You are pigs." Indeed they are, but when they learn to care for themselves, the family is reunited. Humorous illustrations abound with pigs. Try to find all of them! (Ages 4 and up)

Burns, Marilyn. *I Am Not a Short Adult! Getting Good at Being a Kid.* Illustrated by Martha Weston. Boston: Little, Brown, 1977.
This book discusses siblings, responsibility, television, love,

school, and how to decide for yourself what kind of kid you want to be. (Ages 9–12)

Chaikin, Miriam. *A Nightmare in History: The Holocaust 1933–1945.* New York: Clarion Books, 1987. Rogasky, Barbara. *Smoke and Ashes: The Story of the Holocaust.* New York: Holiday House, 1988.

Two well-researched and powerful books on the Holocaust. Both are deftly written, moving accounts that ask readers to bear witness to a terrible time in the history of humankind and to ponder the moral choices involved in being a civilized human being. (Ages 11 and up)

Cohen, Barbara. *Molly's Pilgrim.* Illustrated by Michael J. Dera-ney. New York: Lothrop, Lee & Shepard Books, 1983.

A class learns that not all the pilgrims to our country arrived in the 1620s. A touching story that makes clear the real meaning of Thanksgiving. (Ages 5–9)

Cole, Brock. *The Goats.* New York: Farrar, Straus & Giroux, 1987.

What begins as a cruel prank played on them by their fellow campers turns into an adventure in survival for Howie and Laura as they learn about themselves and each other. An emotionally tense and thoroughly rewarding reading experience that ponders the nature of justice and true intimacy between the sexes. (Ages 11 and up)

Daly, Niki. *Not So Fast, Songololo.* New York: Atheneum, 1986.

A warm, appealing story of a small, black South African boy and his grandmother on a shopping trip to the city. The foreign setting adds a unique message of mutual love between the generations. (Ages 4–7)

Flournoy, Valerie. *The Patchwork Quilt.* Illustrated by Jerry Pink-ney. New York: Dial Books for Young Readers, 1985.

Loving, warm illustrations lend a special luster to the story of Tanya, her grandmother, and the quilt that the whole family helps to finish. (Ages 4–9)

Fox, Mem. *Wilfred Gordon McDonald Partridge.* Illustrated by Julie Vivas. New York: Kane/Miller Books, 1985.

This is a heartwarming story of how a little boy helps an elderly friend regain her lost memory. An import from the Land Down Under that will capture the hearts of American readers of all ages.

Fox, Paula. *One-Eyed Cat: A Novel.* Scarsdale, N.Y.: Bradbury Press, 1984.

Although no one punishes Ned for firing the forbidden air rifle, his conscience troubles him as he cares for the cat he fears he has injured. (Ages 10–14)

Freedman, Florence. *Brothers: A Hebrew Legend.* Illustrated by Robert Andrew Parker. New York: Harper & Row, 1985.

A sweet and poignant retelling of a Hebrew legend that celebrates "How good it is for brothers to live together in friendship." An excellent book to inspire discussion. (Ages 6 and up)

Galdone, Paul. *The Little Red Hen.* New York: Clarion Books, 1979.

Familiar nursery classic about responsibility and sharing the rewards of labor. (Ages 3–5)

Gerstein, Mordicai. *The Mountains of Tibet.* New York: Harper & Row, 1987.

A woodcutter, longing to visit far-off places, grows old and dies without ever having left his village in a Tibetan mountain valley. Offered a chance to live again, the woodcutter must ponder all the possibilities the universe has to offer. Mandala-like art reinforces the thoughtful nature of this picture book for older children. (Ages 6 and up)

Girard, Linda Walvoord. *My Body Is Private.* Illustrated by Rodney Pate. Niles, Ill.: A. Whitman, 1984.

This sensitive, sensible, and careful guide distinguishes between good and bad touching. It emphasizes children's rights to autonomy over their own bodies. (Ages 5–9)

Goble, Paul. *Buffalo Woman*. Scarsdale, N.Y.: Bradbury Press, 1984.

A young hunter marries a female buffalo in the form of a beautiful maiden. When his people reject her, he must pass several tests before being allowed to join the buffalo nation. (Ages 6–10)

Hughes, Shirley. *Alfie Gives a Hand*. New York: Lothrop, Lee & Shepard Books, 1983.

Alfie goes to a birthday party and rescues his friend Min, who is feeling even shyer than he. (Ages 3–6)

Keats, Ezra Jack. *Peter's Chair*. New York: Harper & Row, 1967.

In this classic story, it takes Peter a while to adjust to the idea of a baby sister. (Ages 3–6)

Lobel, Arnold. *Frog and Toad Are Friends*. New York: Harper & Row, 1970.

Childhood classic about friendship, written and illustrated with warmth, wisdom, and humor. (Ages 3–8)

Meltzer, Milton. *Rescue: The Story of How Gentiles Saved Jews in the Holocaust*. New York: Harper & Row, 1988.

Individual acts of heroism and stories about gentiles who defied the Nazis and risked their lives to help the Jews are told with passion in this compelling and inspiring book. (Ages 10–15)

Myers, Walter Dean. *Scorpions*. New York: Harper & Row, 1988.

This Newbery Medal book is a fast-paced story of two best friends, 12-year-old boys, living in a Harlem neighborhood, where kids grow up fast and circumstances are often beyond their control. Provides compelling and hard-hitting reading. (Ages 12–15)

Paulsen, Gary. *Hatchet*. Scarsdale, N.Y.: Bradbury Press, 1987.

Thirteen-year-old Brian is the only survivor of a plane crash, and he must make it on his own in the wilderness with only a hatchet to aid him. This engrossing tale of physical endurance, emotional growth, and the gathering of inner resources is told with great authenticity. (Ages 10–15)

Rogers, Fred. *Making Friends.* Photographed by Jim Judkis. New York: Putnam, 1987.

Mister Rogers explains what it means to be a friend and some of the difficulties and special rewards of friendship. (Ages 2–3)

Dr. Seuss. *Horton Hatches the Egg.* New York: Random House, 1940.

This fun and classic story is about the elephant who is "faithful one hundred per cent," who means what he says, and says what he means. There is no better model of responsibility available. (Ages 4–8)

Siegal, Aranka. *Upon the Head of the Goat: A Childhood in Hungary, 1939–1944.* New York: Farrar, Straus & Giroux, 1981.

The story of 15-year-old Piri, who survived Auschwitz, is movingly recounted in this autobiographical and award-winning novel. She shares the events of her childhood, which formed the basis of the strength and courage that helped her to survive. (Ages 11 and up)

Taylor, Mildred D. *The Friendship.* Illustrated by Max Ginsburg. New York: Dial Books for Young Readers, 1987.

Cassie Logan, heroine of *Roll of Thunder, Hear My Cry,* is sent by her aunt to the Wallace store (a place known to be unfriendly to blacks) to get medicine. There she and her brothers witness a shocking event. This is another story that resonates with meaning and is drawn from the experiences of the author's father. (Ages 10 and up)

Watkins, Yoko Kawashima. *So Far from the Bamboo Grove.* New York: Lothrop, Lee & Shepard Books, 1986.

The author recalls the harrowing close of World War II, when she was separated from her brother and forced to flee Korea for Japan with her mother and older sister. (Ages 12–15)

Weiss, Anne E. *Lies, Deception and Truth.* Boston: Houghton Mifflin, 1988.

Does a good cause justify a lie? Would you lie to help a friend or to save a life? A thought-provoking look at lies—the different types and the reasons behind them. (Ages 10 and up)

Williams, Vera B. *Music, Music for Everyone.* New York: Green-willow Books, 1984.

The money jar is empty and Grandma is sick, so Rosa and her friends form a band to earn money to help with expenses. (Ages 4–7)

Yorinks, Arthur. *Hey, Al.* Illustrated by Richard Egielski. New York: Farrar, Straus & Giroux, 1986.

"Working too hard . . . going nowhere . . . Hey, Al, have I got a place for you," said the large bird to Al, a New York City janitor. So Al and his dog, Eddie, are transported by the bird from their drab apartment to a floating island paradise in the sky. A whimsical fantasy, with the message "Paradise lost is sometimes Heaven found," is brilliantly explored in text and pictures. This Caldecott Medal–winner is a visual, auditory, and philosophical delight. (Ages 4 and up)

Ziefert, Harriet. *Sarah's Questions.* Illustrated by Susan Bonners. New York: Lothrop, Lee & Shepard Books, 1986.

Tired of digging in the garden, Sarah engages her mother in a game of "I Spy," which leads to a series of "why" questions, which, with patience and love, Mother tries to answer. Unhurried tranquil mood is captured in superb, impressionistic illustrations. (Ages 4–8)

# Index

· · · · · ·

# INDEX